Filmguide to

The Rules of the Game

INDIANA UNIVERSITY PRESS FILMGUIDE SERIES
Harry M. Geduld and Ronald Gottesman,
General Editors

Filmguide to

The Rules
of the Game

GERALD MAST

INDIANA UNIVERSITY PRESS
Bloomington London

PN
1997
,R78
M3
1973a

or 9/78

Published in Canada by Fitzhenry & Whiteside Limited, Don Mills, Ontario
Library of Congress catalog card number: 73-75789
ISBN: 0-253-39311-6 cl.   0-253-29312-X pa.
Manufactured in the United States of America

contents

Filmguide to

The Rules of the Game

credits

THE RULES OF THE GAME

Produced by	N.E.F. (La Nouvelle Édition Française)
Scenario and dialogue by	Jean Renoir, with Camille François and Carl Koch
Directed by	Jean Renoir
Assistant directors	André Zwobada, Henri Cartier-Bresson
Music arranged and directed by	Roger Desormières
Script girl	Dido Freire
Director of photography	Jean Bachelet
Camera operator	Jacques Lemare
Assistants	Jean-Paul Alphen, Alain Renoir
Decor	Eugène Lourié
Assistant designer	Max Douy
Costume design	Coco Chanel
Make-up	Ralph
Sound engineer	Joseph de Bretagne
Editing	Marguerite Houlet-Renoir
Assistant editor	Madame Huguet
General manager	Raymond Pillion
Director of production	Claude Renoir
Administrator	Camille François

Time: 110 minutes
Shooting began on February 15, 1939. Filmed on location in Sologne (Chateau de le Ferté–Saint-Aubin, La Motte–Beuvron, Aubigny) and at the Billancourt Studies, Joinville. The film opened on July 7, 1939, in Paris.

CAST

Robert de la Chesnaye	Marcel Dalio
Christine de la Chesnaye	Nora Grégor
André Jurieu	Roland Toutain
Octave	Jean Renoir
Geneviève de Marrast	Mila Parély
Lisette	Paulette Dubost
Schumacher	Gaston Modot
Marceau	Julien Carette
Jackie	Anne Mayen
Saint-Aubin	Pierre Nay
The General	Pierre Magnier
Charlotte	Odette Talazac
The Homosexual	Roger Forster
La Bruyère	Richard Francoeur
Madame de la Bruyère	Claire Gérard
Berthelin	Tony Corteggiani
The South American	Nicolas Amato
Corneille	Eddy Debray
Radio announcer	Lisa Elina
Engineer	André Zwobada
Chef	Léon Larive
Kitchen servant	Célestin

outline

Rules of the Game

1. TITLES

A. Cast and production credits—underscored by a Mozart minuet.
B. Two inserted titles.

1. An announcement that the film is not intended as "social criticism."

2. A crawling title with an excerpt from Beaumarchais' *The Marriage of Figaro,* describing love as inconstant and hearts as meant "to fly."

2. PARIS

A. The night of the aviator's return.

1. André Jurieu arrives at Le Bourget airport after flying the Atlantic alone in his one-engine plane. He tells the radio announcer interviewing him that he is disappointed because "she" hasn't come to meet him and "it's for her I made this flight."

2. Cross-cut to Christine's room, where she is listening to the interview on the radio. She turns it off after André's confession.

3. Return to Le Bourget where Octave counsels André about his foolishness and where an engineer takes over the radio interview with a recitation of the plane's technical specifications.

4. Return to Christine's room where she and her maid, Lisette, discuss love and friendship. Lisette finds friendship with a man an impossibility. Christine walks to her husband's room where Robert de la Chesnaye is also listening to the radio interview. Robert turns off his radio to show Christine another machine—a mechanical music box in the form of a little Negro doll. When Robert tells his wife that he knows that André mistook her friendship for love, she happily tells him that she trusts him absolutely. Robert decides to make a telephone call.

5. Cross-cut to Geneviève's apartment where she receives Robert's call and makes a date to see him next morning. Geneviève rejoins her card-playing guests who are also listening to the radio interview as well as discussing Christine's plight as a foreigner in a strange society.

B. The following days.

1. Robert informs Geneviève that their affair must end, so he can be worthy of his wife.

2. A frantic André smashes his car against an embankment. Octave lectures André on his dangerous foolishness, but when André confesses his genuine pain, Octave offers to help.

3. Octave goes to Christine's house to get André an invitation to the party at La Colinière. At the house, Octave first meets Robert who shows him a mechanical warbler that chirps every twenty seconds. Robert informs Lisette that her husband, Schumacher, wants her to leave Christine's service and live with him. Alone with Christine, Octave tells Christine about André's suicide attempt and asks her to invite him to La Colinière. Christine worries about propriety but eventually agrees to the request, after which she and Octave fall down playfully on her bed. Octave then seeks Robert's permission as well, walking into Robert's room just as he has finished inviting Geneviève to La Colinière. Robert consents to Octave's request for André because he hates walls and wants no barriers between himself and Christine. Octave gleefully plays with one of Robert's musical toys and playfully chases Lisette around the room, after she has brought him a large lunch. Robert searches in the hallway for the lost key to one of his mechanical birds and then returns to his room to tell Octave that Octave is not a fool but a "dangerous poet."

3. ARRIVALS AT LA COLINIÈRE

A. The master arrives.

1. Robert, Christine, and Lisette arrive at the country house in their automobiles. They greet the servants there.

2. Outdoors on the grounds, Schumacher, the gamekeeper, informs Robert of the problems with rabbits on the grounds. Robert tells Schumacher that he does not want any fences around his property and he does not want any rabbits.

3. Schumacher apprehends the poacher, Marceau, in the act and brings him over to Robert. Robert sees the value in Marceau's poaching and hires him to work as his servant. Because of the enmity with Schumacher, Marceau prefers to work inside the house rather than on the grounds.

B. Geneviève arrives.

    1. In a driving rain storm, Geneviève leaves her automobile and enters the house.

    2. Exchanges of greetings between Geneviève and the other guests.

C. André Jurieu arrives.

    1. Christine, in the kitchen, supervises preparation of food for the special tastes and diets of her guests.

    2. She ascends from the kitchen to see André's and Octave's arrival. Exchanges of greetings between the aviator and the guests— while several of the guests gossip about Christine's liaison with the hero. Christine stops their gossip by openly confessing her friendship with André.

D. Marceau arrives.

    1. In the kitchen the servants eat dinner and gossip about their masters.

    2. Marceau clumsily enters the kitchen domain and begins a flirtation with Lisette.

E. The guests retire.

    1. General pleasantries and good-nights in the upstairs corridor.

    2. In more private conversations, Robert thanks Christine for her delicacy, Geneviève tells Octave that she finds the gathering very interesting, and André tells Octave that he is as far from Christine as ever.

4. THE HUNT

A. Preparations.

    1. La Bruyère and Saint-Aubin politely discuss a disputed pheasant.

    2. Schumacher conducts each of the guests to their shooting positions.

    3. Octave tries to console André with the thought that he will eventually forget Christine.

4. The beaters begin to move forward.
B. The slaughter.
1. The frightened rabbits and pheasants begin to scurry out of their cover as the hunters load their guns.
2. Extended sequence of rabbits flipping over and dying, of pheasants plummeting to earth, as the hunters fire.
C. Trophies.
1. As the beaters and dogs pick up the animal corpses, La Bruyère and Saint-Aubin angrily discuss a disputed pheasant. Geneviève pulls Robert aside to speak with him.
2. Berthelin gives Christine a spy glass to look at a squirrel. As Christine surveys the wild life with the glass, she sees Robert and Geneviève embracing—a view which she finds "very interesting."

5. "ENTR'ACTE." BETWEEN THE HUNT AND THE PARTY

A. Christine visits Geneviève's room, where Geneviève is packing. Christine slyly claims to know about Robert's affair with her, "Like everyone else."
1. Christine cleverly discovers that Geneviève knows about Robert's habit of smoking in bed.
2. Christine jovially gets Geneviève to stay for the evening party, claiming that it will divert Robert's eyes from her own activities.
B. Schumacher gives Lisette a new cape, which is practical but "doesn't suit her."
1. Marceau, polishing shoes in the kitchen, chases Lisette flirtatiously around and under a table.
2. Schumacher enters the kitchen and threatens Marceau that next time he will take a shot at him.
3. Corneille, the major-domo, orders the disruptive Schumacher out of the kitchen.

6. THE PARTY

A. The couples sneak off.
1. Christine pulls Saint-Aubin away from the other performers on stage at the party, and Geneviève pulls Robert away from the group.

2. Skeletons and the figure of death dance on a black stage, accompanied by Saint-Saëns' *Danse macabre.* In the flickering shadows of the room, Marceau embraces Lisette, as Schumacher searches for his wife; in the shadows, Christine sits with Saint-Aubin, observed by André. While Octave searches for someone to help him remove his bearskin costume, André and Robert search for Christine and Schumacher continues to search for Lisette. Robert helps Marceau avoid his pursuer, Schumacher, and in their conversation Robert yearns for the Moslem way of dealing with women but Marceau finds that the only solution is to make them laugh.

B. The "duels."

1. Schumacher unwittingly opens the door of the gun room, revealing Christine in Saint-Aubin's arms. André demands to know what Christine is doing. When Saint-Aubin challenges André to a duel, André kicks him up the backside. In the fight, Jackie, Christine's niece, who adores André, faints, Saint-Aubin is knocked out, and André returns to speak to Christine. She confesses that she loves him and the two plan to leave together. André first wants to explain to Robert because "there are certain rules."

2. Cross-cut to the stage performance at the party, where the Homosexual, Berthelin, La Bruyère, and the South American sing, "We've Raised One Foot." Robert then introduces his newest mechanical toy—a huge organ with dazzling lights and mechanical musicians. Robert beams with excited pride as the machine plays.

3. Schumacher looks for Marceau in the kitchen. Lisette covers up for Marceau by giving her husband some wine and pretending that she will go off with him to Alsace. Marceau, sneaking off, knocks over a tray, and Schumacher leaps back to the chase— which even the commands of Robert cannot halt.

4. Return to André and Christine, who tells the aviator that she will leave with him immediately or not at all. Robert, chasing Schumacher, discovers his wife and André in the gun room. When André tries to explain, Robert punches him in the face—and the second brawl begins. During the brawl, Christine flees the room with Octave and Geneviève watches with drunken dispassion. Schumacher, chasing Marceau through the gun room, waves a pistol.

When the shot rings out, Robert instantly ceases the brawl with André and Geneviève begins shrieking hysterically.

5. Return to Christine and Octave. Octave recalls his fond memories of Christine's famous father—an important conductor. Octave strides out of the house and onto the balcony to conduct an invisible orchestra. He realizes that his dream of power is merely an illusion.

6. Cross-cut to Schumacher chasing Marceau through the salon, where Schumacher continues to fire his pistol. The guests think the shooting is merely part of the evening's entertainment. Schumacher holds all the guests at gun point in the salon as the mechanical organ goes berserk. Corneille trips up Schumacher, takes the pistol, and ends the chase.

7. AFTER THE PARTY

A. Sorting out the couples.

1. Robert and André put the screeching Geneviève and fainting Jackie to bed. Robert bids good night to the guests, discovers from Corneille that there has been only minor damage, and discharges both Schumacher and Marceau for the disruption. Robert and André apologize to each other for acting like peasants. Robert loves Christine so much he will let her go with André.

2. Cross-cut to Christine and Octave, who tells her that André is a hero in the air and a fool on the ground. Both Octave and Lisette admit they knew about Robert's affair with Geneviève but wanted to spare Christine's feelings. When Christine remarks that her life has been based on a lie, Octave counters that it is an era when everyone lies. Lisette gives Christine the cape that Schumacher bought for her.

3. Marceau meets a weeping Schumacher on the grounds. Whereas Marceau plans to go back to poaching on a legal basis, with a hunting license, Schumacher plans to get Lisette back from "them."

4. Octave confesses to Christine that he is a failure and a parasite. Schumacher sees the couple in the distance and believes that Octave is "poaching" Lisette (because of the cape). In the greenhouse, Christine tells Octave that she really loves him.

Schumacher goes for his rifle as Octave goes back to the house for his coat, preparing to leave with Christine on the next train.

   5. In the chateau, Robert and André note that Christine is with Octave so there is nothing to worry about. As Octave searches for his hat, Lisette convinces Octave that it is wrong for him to take Christine away. Octave tells André that Christine is "waiting for you," and André rushes off with Octave's overcoat.

   6. Schumacher mistakes André for Octave in the darkness and fires. André pitches forward and dies, softly calling Christine's name. Schumacher and Marceau both recognize their error. Marceau runs to the house to inform Robert, Octave, Jackie, and Lisette. Lisette bids goodbye to both Marceau and Octave; she and Corneille rush off to help the masters. Octave and Marceau bid farewell—Marceau to return to his poaching and Octave to his "poaching" in Paris.

B. The return to the chateau.

   1. The weary and tearful masters, supported by their servants, return to the house. Robert gives Schumacher instructions for Corneille, who will deal with the formalities. Christine tells Jackie to brace up because "people are looking at you." The women enter the house first as Christine politely bids good night to her guests.

   2. Robert announces that "a regrettable accident" has occurred —that his keeper, Schumacher, thought he saw a poacher and fired, as was his duty. Robert delivers a brief eulogy to André, "who could make us forget he was a famous man." He bids them all retire for the night. Although Saint-Aubin sarcastically notes the new definition of "accident," the General approves, for Robert has shown that he has "class," a rare quality these days.

   3. As the shadows of the guests drift into the chateau, the camera holds on the exterior of the house. The word *Fin* dissolves into the frame as the Mozart minuet concludes on the sound track.

the director

The Works of Jean Renoir

Jean Renoir is one of the few film directors to be acknowledged an artistic master by all schools of film criticism—literary, auteurist, humanist, scholarly, popularist, sociological, and technical. Renoir's films seem to satisfy everyone's notions of what a great work of film art should be: interesting story, vital characters, brilliant acting, social criticism, poetic symbolism, philosophical observation, structural complexity, and stunning visual compositions. Renoir films are excitingly entertaining and compellingly intellectual at the same time. In an astonishingly long career (1924–69) no other director of films (with the obvious exception of Chaplin) has created so many works of such consistent high quality and so few works that require apology or rationalization from admirers.

Renoir's unique artistic position is a product of the uniqueness of the artist himself. Renoir's dominant artistic and intellectual trait is his doubleness, a multiplicity and ambivalence that allow him to see more than one side of every question and in more than one direction at any time. What Renoir loses in the passionate single-ness of vision of many directors, a singleness that usually allows them to make only one or two great films, he gains in the many-sidedness of his vision that (like Shakespeare and Dickens and Ibsen) allows him to express his artistic consciousness through a large number of external forms.

Renoir is both optimist and pessimist, romantic and ironist, cynic and mystic. Although he is a pure man of the cinema, his cinema is often dependent on the conventions of the theatre (that supposed foe of the cinematic), the shapes and shading of painting (which he inherits from his famous father), and the tones and rhythms of music. Renoir has that historical sense that allows him to see the past in the present and the present in the past, the sociological sense that allows him to see the same men in different cultures and different men in the same cultures, and the dramatic sense that allows him to see the farce of tragedy and the tragedy in farce. He is one of those artists who can assert a position passionately and then add his own, "Yes, but. . . ."

This doubleness and ambivalence spans Renoir's entire career. His central thematic contrast is between nature and society, the spontaneity of natural human responses and the stifling regulations of civilization. *Boudu sauvé des eaux* (*Boudu Saved from Drowning,* 1932) is a conflict between the absolute man of nature, Boudu, and the absolute man of society, Lestingois, a bourgeois businessman who, appropriately, sells books, society's ultimate testament to itself. *Les Bas-Fonds* (*The Lower Depths,* 1936) contrasts life in a stifling social microcosm and the freedom of life in the fields and open air. *Une Partie de Campagne* (*A Day in the Country,* 1936) contrasts the lives of city people and country people. *The Southerner* (1945), made in the United States, contrasts life in the vicious city with the freedom of life on the farm. And *Le Déjeuner sur l'herbe* (*Picnic on the Grass,* 1959) farcically depicts the conflict between a politician who is so artificial that he believes in artificial insemination and country people who believe in spontaneous, natural sexual experience.

But Renoir's view of nature is never as simple and as singleminded as many of his critics claim. In *Boudu,* for example, although the director's and the audience's sympathies are obviously with Boudu, the vital, spontaneous man of nature, Renoir realizes that there is plenty of Lestingois in himself and everyone else as well. Like Lestingois, Renoir is a man of society, not an isolated tramp. Indeed, filmmaking is the most social of all the arts, requiring a whole society of people (both behind and before a camera) to make a film, and a whole society to watch it. Renoir, like Lestingois, turns nature into art. Just as Lestingois poeticizes love into pastoral terms (Pan, Priapus, and the like), Renoir poeticizes the natural (e.g., a tree) into the artificial (an image on celluloid). There is a similar ambivalence in *La Petite Marchande d'allumettes* (*The Little Match Girl,* 1928), *Toni* (1935), *La Grande Illusion* (*Grand Illusion,* 1937), *Swamp Water* (1941), *The Southerner, The Woman on the Beach* (1947), and *The River* (1951) in which nature is not simply benign but can be savage and murderous as well. This duality between the chaotic spontaneity of nature and the orderly precision of social rules produces much of the ambiguity, richness, and complexity of *The Rules of the Game.*

Yet another related Renoir concern is the contrast between nature (or life as it is lived and experienced) and art (or the conversion of life into an artifact). And again Renoir can see the validity of both choices. Whereas *Boudu* looks cynically at culture's ability to transform itself into meaningful works of art (Lestingois' books), *Le Crime de M. Lange* (*The Crime of M. Lange,* 1936) shows that writing novels and making films about a lengendary American cowboy, "Arizona Jim," can transform a vicious capitalistic business into a human, humane, happy communal activity, even if the activity is so artificial that none of the creators has ever been to Arizona. Both *Grand Illusion* and *The Rules of the Game* contain their own ambivalence, for both depict elegant societies that have, in a sense, turned themselves into works of art (the French and German nobility of *Grand Illusion,* the society at La Colinière in *Rules of the Game*), but not without murdering human spontaneity (quite literally) in the process.

The later Renoir films are most specifically occupied with the conflicting claims of art and nature. The central figure of *Le Carosse d'or* (*The Golden Coach,* 1953) is an actress, Camilla, who finds it impossible to confine herself to a single lover or a single life-style. The stage permits a person to experience an infinity of lovers and life-styles. Camilla loves the stage more than her lovers, and she loses her lovers as a result. Although she has some regrets, she realizes that the only place where she is most fully alive is on the stage. Similarly, in *French Cancan* (1955) a nightclub entrepreneur, Danglard, reveals that only by being a faithless and fickle lover can he produce great works of art. Danglard uses women as objects to be molded into performing artists, not as human beings to be loved. Love is a means, not an end; he loves the dance, not any dancer. Althuogh the producer's manipulations may seem callous and inhuman, they define his being and his existence as an artist.

These late Renoir films reveal a kind of spiritual progression in the filmmaker's view of art, of himself, and of his relation to the society of others. Renoir's personal conflicts and commitments had always played a major role in his films. It is possible to see *Boudu sauvé des eaux* as representing Renoir's internal conflict as a younger man—the longing to be a Boudu, yet the consciousness that he is really a Lestingois. There is a sense of despair, self-loathing, and self-doubt in the Renoir films of the 1930s—almost as if the filmmaker realizes that the world is running amok and all he can do is to make his elegant little films that cannot change or help anybody or anything. Most of Renoir's 1930s films contain deaths—among them, *La Chienne* (1931), *Toni, The Crime of M. Lange, The Lower Depths, Grand Illusion, The Rules of the Game*—many of those deaths being useless or unjust, often bitterly unnecessary or brutally comic.

The climax of this decade of self-doubt is Renoir's playing a failure and parasite, Octave, in *The Rules of the Game.* Renoir had acted in five of his earlier films, playing such contemptible roles as pimp, wolf, and poacher. But Octave is a culmination of self-doubt, for he is a failure as both a man and an artist. Instead of becoming a great conductor, he has become a gluttonous sponger; he is too cowardly to elope with the woman he loves; and he is such a clumsy manipulator of human events (which, ironically, is precisely the business of a filmmaker) that he sends his best friend off to his death.

But the Renoir films of the 1950s lack the sense of death and failure. Both *The Golden Coach* and *French Cancan* proclaim that the truly committed, successful artist necessarily makes himself successful as a human being, and both *Elena et les hommes* (1956) and *Picnic on the Grass* look at political problems more humorously, lightly, and "operettically" than Renoir's political films of the 1930s. Perhaps the dominant attitude of these late films descends from Renoir's first film of the decade, *The River* (1951), which was also the first film he made after returning to France from the United States (where Renoir lived and directed during the war and just after it) and the first film he made in color.

The River was shot on location in India, using Western and Indian actors, both amateurs and professionals. To some extent, the process of making the film (a Western director and staff working within the Indian culture) is also its subject, the story of Westerners who live in the midst of Indian culture and who take from that culture its wisdom, its reverence for nature, and its assumption that man is somehow a part of the scheme of the universe—like the trees, the animals, and the river itself. The film contrasts the chaos of the West (one of the characters is an American who lost a leg in the war) with the serenity of Indian life; it contrasts the fact of death (one child dies from a cobra's bite) with the fact of life (another baby is born as the film ends); it contrasts the beauty of nature (the Ganges) with the transformation of nature into art (the river is a religious object as well as a natural one; it inspires artistic myths as well as the vital music of the sitar which mirrors its rhythms).

After the child's death, the American soldier, in a moment of despair, questions the girl, who is a synthesis of the film's values. Her father is Western and her mother Indian.

> "What do we do?"
> "Consent."
> "To what?"
> "To everything."

Although one cannot ever smooth out the ambivalence and intentional self-contradiction in the work of Renoir, his artistic career seems to be a journey from conflict to consent.

Jean Renoir is as remarkable for his cinema technique as his complex thought. Film theorist André Bazin credits Renoir with discovering and developing one of the essential tools of sound films, the composition in depth, using depth-of-field photography to produce contrast, tension, and information in the relationship of foreground and rearground. Almost a decade before Orson Welles' famed use of depth-of-field in *Citizen Kane,* Renoir was using such deep-focus photography, shooting scenes through windows and doors (or out of windows and doors), revealing some relationship between events and characters close to the camera and distant from it at the same time. In *A Day in the Country,* for example, two men eat their lunch in the kitchen while two women sit outside the window on swings in the sunlight. The shot instantly links the men and women spiritually and prepares for the meeting of the two couples, which becomes the basis of the film's plot. The shot also contrasts the two regions—indoor confinement and outdoor spontaneity— that underlie that plot.

The shot is also interesting visually in its own right. One of the difficulties of sound films in the early years was to combine talking with interesting, vital compositions so that the film remained a *motion* picture. Renoir's compositions in depth remain constantly interesting to the eye; they never allow talk to dominate the visual but to coexist with it as an equal and ally. Because montage (editing), one of the essential tools of the silent film, distracted the audience from the dialogue and distorted the social interaction in a film by leaping around, Renoir's use of depth-of-field kept his dialogue films visually alive.

The technique also allows the audience to pick out the important pieces of human information for itself. Given the subtlety and complexity of Renoir's thought and psychological observation, his essential means of communication was implication. Rather than shoving his points at the audience, which montage necessarily does by forcing attention on the individual pieces, Renoir forces the member of the auidence to infer the significant points by selecting and adding up the pieces for himself. This method supports the subtlety and tonal consistency of his films since it never overstates or overemphasizes—another of the dangers of montage.

In addition to this dominant compositional method, Renoir was a master of visual imagery, constantly allowing the shot's content and atmosphere to speak for him without resorting to overexplanatory dialogue. The harsh, bright landscapes of *Toni,* the claustrophobic interiors of *The Lower Depths,* the contrast of snow and stone in *Grand Illusion,* the fields in *The Southerner,* the desolate beach in *The Woman on the Beach,* the river and river life in *The River* all said so much that the characters needed to say much less. The reliance on imagery further contributed to Renoir's subtle style by demanding inferences rather than by explicitly stating the issues.

Renoir was as attentive to the devices of sound as he was to the visual. His ear for exactly the right music for a film—music which not only supported the film's tone and rhythms but also underscored its intellectual issues—was uncanny. In *Boudu sauvé des eaux*'s contrast of natural and bourgeois man, Renoir used music both to define Boudu (an inarticulate grunting song) and his bourgeois antagonists (a military marching band; the saccharine strains of the "Blue Danube" waltz). The film also uses a mellow and reedy flute to link the sequences, a light musical touch that adds an airiness to the film's tone because of its delicacy and because it does not fit precisely on either side of the film's intellectual argument.

In *Toni* Renoir uses the fiery guitar music and folk songs of the Spanish peasants, which underscore the spirit and passions of the film's people. *Grand Illusion* weaves several songs into its plot— "Frou, Frou, Frou" (to define the French camp); a Strauss waltz (to define the German one); "The Marseillaise" (which the French prisoners sing inside the German prison); "Il était un petit navire" (which the French captain plays on his little flute to aid the two escaping prisoners and which later serves to mend those two men's feelings after an argument). *The River* effectively uses the sitar to define the Indian culture and the film's spirit; *The Golden Coach* uses the music of Vivaldi to underscore the grace of the Spanish aristocrats and the graceful conventions of the acting troupe's *Commedia dell' arte; French Cancan* uses the vibrant music of the dance and the lilting ballads of Montmartre. *Picnic on the Grass* contrasts the sterile politicians and the vibrant provincials by using cacaphonous, percussive jazz rhythms for the politicians and mellow reed instruments for the people. In both *Boudu* and *Picnic on the Grass* the wind instruments contain the breath of life.

When Renoir turned to color cinematography in 1950, he used color "musically" as he had previously used music for tonal coloring. Color became an ally of music in these films, casting a tonal spell on the film's events, people, and themes. *The River* comes alive with its shots of the blue-gray-green Ganges, the red dust of the soil, the sharp greens, whites, yellows, and reds of the Indian villages, houses, and foliage. For *The Golden Coach* Renoir parallels the Vivaldi sound with the warm, rich colors of baroque painting—deep browns, ripe reds, burnished gold—the perfect visual accompaniment for the film's setting, period, story, and music. *French Cancan* accompanies the music of Montmartre with the pastels of impressionist painting—pale blues, greens, pinks, and lavenders. In his use of sound as color and color as music Renoir achieved a degree of tonal harmony and visual communication that has never been surpassed and has only been equalled (occasionally) by Michelangelo Antonioni, who made this kind of synesthesia the basis of his entire technique.

Finally, another of Renoir's directorial gifts is his ability with actors, his ability to turn performances into rich human portraits. Despite the structural complexity and intellectual clarity of Renoir's scripts, his films begin with people and are built around them. Renoir speaks of changing whole scripts because of the presence of such gifted actors as Erich von Stroheim and Anna Magnani. The vibrant presence of dynamic performers adds human flesh to the structural bones of Renoir's intellectual conceptions, ultimately making his films, which are supremely complicated works of artifice, seem like life. Not only does Renoir use many of the greatest film actors, but many of them have never been better than in his films: Michel Simon (in *Boudu*), Jean Gabin (in *The Lower Depths, Grand Illusion,* and *French Cancan*), Erich von Stroheim (in *Grand Illusion*), Marcel Dalio (in *Grand Illusion* and *The Rules of the Game*), and Anna Magnani (in *The Golden Coach*).

As works of film art, Renoir's films seem themselves to represent the same kinds of syntheses that are their subjects: the synthesis of life and art, thought and feeling, talk and picture, spontaneity and construction, individual and whole.

production

The History of *The Rules of the Game*

The history of *The Rules of the Game* (*La Règle du jeu*) reads more like melodrama. The film hung on the brink of disaster from the beginning. First, Renoir could not afford Simone Simon whom he really wanted to play Christine, and the resulting change to Nora Grégor still clouds the film in ambiguity and perhaps even has changed its intended meaning. Then, the shooting of the film went slowly, hampered by poor weather, the need to improvise scenes because of the difficulties with Nora Grégor, and the gloomy mood of impending war which hung over the entire production.

When the film was released it evoked derisive hoots and even riots in the Paris theatres. The right-wing press was especially hostile to the film, considering it a slap at French culture and tradition in general and deploring its cynical treatment of snobbery and anti-Semitism in the working classes. Renoir kept cutting the pieces out of the film where the audience booed—eventually eliminating almost twenty minutes—but the audience continued to boo in new places at each showing. Despite Renoir's cuts the film was picketed by a right-wing Catholic organization wherever it was shown. Eventually the film was banned by the French government even before the fall of France for being "demoralizing." The German occupation government banned the film again (they also banned *Grand Illusion*). And during the war an allied bombing attack destroyed the laboratories where the complete negative of the original version of the film had been stored.

A last-minute rescue seemed impossible. Two multilated, short versions of the film circulated just after the war, but it was impossible to assess the film's full value, structure, and intentions from them. Then two enterprising film buffs, Jean Gaborit and Jacques Durand, bought the rights to the film and collected hundreds of cans of film from all over the world, eventually assembling (with

Renoir's help) a nearly complete print of the film that omitted only one brief scene of the original. The newly assembled print premiered at the Venice Film Festival of 1959 (*Grand Illusion* had enjoyed a similar reassembling and had premiered at the Brussels World's Fair of 1958). Since 1959 *The Rules of the Game* has appeared on almost every "top ten best film of all time" list, placing third in the international *Sight and Sound* poll of 1962, second in the 1972 poll. The film had finally been rescued from oblivion.

Renoir formed his own production company for *The Rules of the Game*. He had had difficulties in making films for established production companies, having acquired a reputation for extravagance in the 1920s and for controversy in the 1930s. As his own producer, he would not have to worry about cutting material from his film (as he had with *La Bête humaine* in 1938) to suit others. Renoir and four partners, Camille François, Claude Renoir (his younger brother), André Zwobada, and Oliver Billiou, combined to form the N.E.F.—La Nouvelle Édition Française. The N.E.F.'s goal was to produce two features a year. The financial problems of *The Rules of the Game* and the fall of France confined this short-lived company's output to the single film.

Renoir assembled a team of collaborators for the film with whom he had worked often and well (just as most successful directors have worked with a regular team of writers and technicians— Griffith, Eisenstein, Lubitsch, Hawks, Carné, DeSica, Bergman, Antonioni, Fellini, etc.). Renoir wrote his own script, assisted by Carl Koch (who had collaborated with Renoir on *Grand Illusion* and *La Marseillaise*), Jean Bachelet photographed the film (he had photographed *Madame Bovary, The Crime of M. Lange,* and *The Lower Depths*), and Marguerite Renoir (Renoir's mistress, who adopted his name) edited the film (she had edited every Renoir film since *La Chienne* in 1931).

The script and concept of *The Rules of the Game* altered considerably in the course of shooting, primarily because of the strengths of several of the players and the weakness of Nora Grégor. Originally, the film was to contain far more material about Christine's famous father, named Stiller, and his relationship with Robert de la Chesnaye, material which in the finished film is only briefly alluded to by Octave and is more closely related to his own hopes and feelings than anyone else's. Originally, Robert de la Chesnaye was to be a patron of the arts and music rather than a collector of mechanical artifacts and canned music boxes. Christine was originally planned as a bored woman of the world who has nothing to do but plan parties, rather than a woman who doesn't seem particularly bored or particularly worldly and who doesn't plan a single party. The roles of Lisette, Marceau, Schumacher, and Geneviève were originally much smaller and less important in Renoir's conception, but the abilities of the performers (Paulette Dubost's energetic and bouncy Lisette; Carette's clownish and Chaplinesque Marceau; Gaston Modot's stern Schumacher; and Mila Parély's haunting and vibrant Geneviève) expanded their parts in the course of shooting. Renoir calls *The Rules of the Game* his most improvised film, an astounding fact considering that the finished product is as perfectly and precisely structured as one of Robert's clockwork dolls.

The film's first major setback was Renoir's inability to secure the seductive and sensual Simone Simon to play Christine. She had recently been to Hollywood and returned to France with higher salary demands than the N.E.F. company could meet. Renoir settled instead on an amateur actress, Nora Grégor, who was a European socialite (also known as the Princess Starhemberg) and who attracted him with her cold mysteriousness. What the film would have been like with the warm siren, Simon, rather than the inexplicably cold Grégor is a matter of conjecture, but much of the film's ambiguity, ambivalence, and richness is undoubtedly a product of the unfathomable, uncommitted, and unclear coldness of Christine, which becomes either an intentional or accidental virtue in the film's fabric. Another casting shift, far more fortunate for the film, was Renoir's decision to play Octave himself (originally his elder brother, Pierre, was to have played the role). Renoir explained that no one could play Octave with more docility than himself.

Another change, which certainly would have influenced the final work, was Renoir's abandoning the idea of shooting the film in Technicolor. The Technicolor company was interested in the project, and Renoir was interested in color (as his films of the 1950s would show), particularly since he thought the forests of

Sologne admirably suited to color filming. Renoir needed the Technicolor company to agree to pay for all expenses beyond the expected budget for a black-and-white production, but Technicolor could not make a commitment before shooting was scheduled to begin.

Shooting began on February 15, 1939, on location in Sologne, Renoir filming the outdoor sequences first. The company then returned to the Pathé studio near Paris for the indoor sequences. The original fine cut of the film ran 113 minutes, which Renoir cut to 100 minutes at the request of Gaumont, the film's distributors. The film opened on July 7, 1939, at two theatres in Paris. In an effort to soften the hostility of both audiences and critics, Renoir successively cut the film to 90 minutes, then to 85. The film was withdrawn from circulation after about a week.

Not until twenty years later did Les Grands Films Classiques company (Messrs. Gaborit and Durand, with the aid and advice of Jacques Maréchal and Joseph Kosma) rescue *The Rules of the Game* from public hostility, critical condemnation, government blacklists, Allied bombs, and commercial multilation. The present version of 110 minutes contains all the material of Renoir's original except for a brief discussion between André and Octave during the hunt in which Octave states a preference for serving women to upper-class ladies.

analysis

The structure of *The Rules of the Game* is a descendant of the French theatre of the eighteenth century. An opening title quotes Beaumarchais, one of the comic dramatists of that century, and throughout the film there are echoes of other dramatic works—by Beaumarchais, Marivaux, and de Musset, also Molière and the farceur Feydeau, even Shakespeare and Jonson, and indeed many of the masters of classical comedy. (It is no accident that the film's major-domo, one of the figures of competence and order, is named Corneille, one of the great masters of French classical tragedy who placed duty before passion.)

The film manipulates the devices of classical comedy. There are parallel actions of masters and servants, the activities in the lower classes being a "vulgar" and low-comic mirror of those in the upper ones. As in the classical comedy, the subject matter is love—requited and unrequited; requited and then unrequited; unrequited and then requited—as well as the consequent errors of love—jealousy, misinterpretation, and misunderstanding. There are even such classical comic devices as the interwoven chase (various lovers weaving in and out of rooms searching for their own beloved), the mistaken identity arising from a piece of clothing (Lisette's cloak and Octave's raincoat), and the farcical slap in the face and kick up the backside (the fights between André and Saint-Aubin, André and Robert).

Most like the classical theatre, the film is built in five acts—like any traditional French play. The overall structure of the film, like the classical comedy, is to introduce the individual human pieces in the early acts, to bring them together shortly thereafter, to scramble them in the middle acts, and then to sort them out for the conclusion. The great difference, of course, between Renoir's film and classical comedy—a difference which he deliberately manipulates—is that his film contains many events, characters, themes, and social implications not usually found in a traditional comedy. Whereas the traditional comedy often ends with a party and a dance (think of Shakespeare's *A Midsummer Night's Dream*), Renoir chooses not to end his film with a party but to add a serious, melancholy, and catastrophic act after the party ends. Inspired juxtaposition of serious material and comic devices is ultimately what gives *The Rules of the Game* its dramatic power, its human complexity, its intellectual richness, and its reputation as one of the greatest works of film art of all time.

Cinematically, Renoir's technique in the film is also allied with the stage, but such is Renoir's cinematic sense that he can convert the completely theatrical into the completely cinematic. *The Rules of the Game* is no stilted, talky film that seems more like "canned theatre" than cinema. This synthesis of cinema and theatre returns to Renoir's later work with *The Golden Coach* and *French Cancan;* it also influences such filmed masterpieces as Carné-Prévert's *The Children of Paradise* and Max Ophuls' *Lola Montès,* which also combine the theatrical with the cinematic with equal effectiveness. Most of *The Rules of the Game* takes place indoors, in various "drawing rooms," like any drawing-room comedy. The few sequences that take place outdoors (most memorably the hunting scene) do not, however, feel freer or cinematically more inventive than the indoor ones but seem of a piece with the indoor work. Renoir achieves this unity by using the same dominant techniques—primarily the moving camera and the shot-in-depth—for both indoor and outdoor sequences.

The large number of tracking shots in the film (perhaps half the film's 337 shots are tracking shots) keep the film alive visually and also allow Renoir to record important dialogue sequences in lengthy takes (many are almost a minute long) that neither divert attention from the speakers nor allow the film to bog down in laborious talk. Renoir's indoor shots in depth (down the long corridors, inside drawing rooms as two characters converse) similarly divert the eye without diverting attention from the talk. The film's control of tonal lighting, its visual contrasts of various rooms and locations, its effective use of silence and music, its costumes (designed by Coco

Chanel), and its vigorous performances all contribute to turning an extremely theatrical piece into magnificent cinema.

ACT 1

The first act takes place in Paris on the evening of the aviator's landing at Le Bourget and the days following it. As exposition, the act is a marvel of artistic economy, introducing the audience to every major character (except Marceau), the film's central terms (love, marriage, friendship, and desire), the film's social milieu (the gossip, the hypocrisy, and the assumptions about propriety), and the fact that these people are attempting to live in the graceful "old" style in the midst of a world dominated by machines (the contrast between the modern radio, airplane, telephone, and automobile, and Robert's antique mechanical animals and dolls). The first act plants almost every detail that will function later in the film, including Octave's attachment to his raincoat.

The first sequence—André's arrival and its reception by Christine, Robert, and Geneviève—is dominated by the device of the radio, which links Le Bourget with all three rooms. The film begins with coils of cable, plunging us immediately into the modern world of machines. The camera tracks down the length of cable, a kind of mechanical umbilical cord, to the announcer at the end of it, holding her microphone. The whole texture of the opening scene is one of push, noise, and bustle. There are crowd noises on the sound track; the announcer's voice is nasal and rasping; her determination to push through both the crowd and the police is almost barbarically impolite. Interestingly, Renoir creates the impression of bustle and crowds with the use of the cinema alone; at no time do more than a few dozen people appear in the frame. But with his bustling tracking shots, his tight compositions on the announcer's face, the impression that both she and the camera are bits of flotsam in a human sea which can be felt but not seen, Renoir creates the atmosphere of the scene without resorting to hundreds of extras. The scene takes place in darkness, which converts the crowd into vague flickers of light in the dark and establishes the dark mood of the film (the film ends in darkness as well).

André's interview with the announcer, after his warm and sincere meeting with Octave (an embrace establishes Octave's sincere friendliness), is the film's first clash between the demands of the private and the public, those private, personal emotions that a human being feels as opposed to the external, social demands on human behavior. Rather than confining himself to the expected sentiments of a public hero, André expresses his disappointment that the woman he loves has not come to meet him. To emphasize the moment, Renoir holds his camera on André's face, deleting both the camera and background movement that had so dominated the previous shots; he also quiets the noises of the crowd and adds a slight pause before André leaps into his social *faux pas,* emphasizing the feeling of the event still more.

The interview with the dry engineer that follows reveals the same kind of contrast between form and feeling. The engineer reduces the human exertion of André's performance to a simple matter of the mechanical capabilities and the fuel tanks of the machine. Ironically, one of André's first words upon arrival was that the machine, and not the man, should be given the credit. The important fact for André was not that he flew a machine but that he flew to the woman he loved.

Intercut among the scenes at the airport are scenes in Christine's room; she has been listening to the interview. Interestingly, Renoir begins her scenes with a shot of the tubes of her radio; as in the opening shot of the film, he begins with the apparatus and then tracks with the camera to link the machine to the people. Christine's room is in deliberate visual contrast with the scenes at the airport— brightly lit rather than dark, ornately decorated with curtains, silks, mirrors, bottles, and crystal rather than the stark bareness of the airport scene. In his switch from the public to the most private domain (the bedroom), Renoir then engages the lady and her servant in the most private of subjects, triggered by André's beginning a discussion of that subject in public.

The parallels between Madame and her maid become clear quite early. Both women are married (Lisette for two years, Christine for three); both women have relationships with men other than their husbands. But Christine seems to feel that friendship with a man is a possibility, whereas Lisette finds it as impossible as "discussing the moon in broad daylight." (The film's subtitles are woefully inadequate with Lisette's metaphor.) Lisette's feelings about the subject of sex and friendship are clear; Christine's are not. Indeed the vagueness and the mysteriousness about Christine's feelings, attitudes, and even attractiveness begin in this first scene. Renoir shoots much of the scene with Christine's face reflected in her dressing-table mirror. Here Renoir uses the surrounding decor—the glass, the ornate bed curtains, the elaborate shapes and textures of the room itself—to mirror the woman's tastes and values, much as Ophuls uses decor and mirrors in the opening sequence of *Madame de . . . .* But in addition to capturing Christine's mirrored face, the camera also depicts her immensely broad, bony, and un-alluring back, harshly exposed by a backless evening dress. The impression of gawky unattractiveness and Christine's stooped shoulders increases when she rises from the table to walk down the hall, a walk totally lacking in grace, fluidity, or evocative charm. Why is Christine, the siren who bewitches four men in the course of the film, so unattractive? The question has no answer at this point of the film (and perhaps will never have one), but the tension and mysteriousness in the character of Christine is established early.

Renoir links Christine's room with Robert's by a tracking shot, following Christine as she leaves her room and walks toward her husband's. The use of deep-focus photography in the long corridor also establishes the size of the house and Madame's relationship to her servants. For example, she depends on Corneille to know the master's whereabouts exactly at all times.

Robert too is listening to the radio; the interview has concluded and the announcer is about to sign off. Robert turns off the one machine and shows his wife another, a little mechanical Negress, whose "mechanism is perfect." Renoir then chooses to isolate the music box itself, shooting it in an extreme close-up. Its little head moves back and forth and it emits a tinkling musical tune. The doll is both cute and grotesque, pretty and ugly, living and dead. Indeed, it contains the same kind of synthesis as the radio: it imitates human life and appears to be alive, but it is really a soulless, dead apparatus. Although no moral inference can yet be drawn from either the radio or the doll (both are inanimate and marvelous at the same time), it is clear that both contain precisely the same kind of tension between life and death. Christine's response to the doll shows how deliberate Renoir's parallel is: "I like it better than the radio."

Her mentioning the radio naturally leads Robert to a discussion of Christine's relationship with André Jurieu; he wants to tell her both that he knows about the relationship and that he trusts her. To underline the delicacy of Robert's admission and the slight discomfort of the subject matter, Renoir shoots Robert's speech with another moving shot, following Robert as he walks, the movement of both man and camera mirroring the tension of the topic. Later Renoir will use the same camera strategy when Robert agrees to let Octave bring André to La Colinière.

Robert makes his open admission to Christine for the same reason that he invites André later—he does not believe in fences, in barriers between himself and his wife. He wants to be open and honest about what he knows. Ironically, Robert, like almost everyone else, knows about Christine's secret, just as almost everyone (except Christine) knows about Robert's. So whereas André's social sin at the airport is to make public what should be kept private, it turns out that even what is private is indeed public information. One only pretends that it is private by not acknowledging the public knowledge publicly. This irony, that the private passions are not truly private but that everyone in public pretends that they are, is one of the central issues around which the film turns.

Christine's response to Robert's openness is apparently relief and gratitude. "Oh! I'm so happy! Thank you!" And she spins energetically in a circle. But the response rings strangely—not false, but not quite true either. First, the physical turn is clumsy and, like her walking, one of Nora Grégor's least fortunate physical moments in the film. Second, beneath the surface of her line Christine doesn't seem particularly happy or relieved, nor does she seem to be lying, nor does she seem to be implying something else. She seems to imply little at all, despite her explicit statement. There is a gap between the sub-text (the underlying emotions for which the text is merely a summarization and external manifestation) and text in the remark. Is it an intentional or unintentional gap?

Christine then tells Robert that a lie is a heavy garment to carry around—a metaphor which introduces the imagery of clothing to the film. Ironically, in the film's climax the characters will indeed wear garments that lie about the identities of the wearers. Christine's

assertion that she trusts Robert absolutely sends him scurrying back
to his study, for he is wearing his own lie (and the moving camera
follows him to increase the sense of agitation). In his study, Robert
uses the telephone, yet another machine, while reflected in an ornate
mirror (as was his wife earlier). As he converses, he toys with
another mechanical music box (keeping the presence of the mechanical perpetually before the audience). Throughout the film
Robert occupies himself with his machines at his most vulnerable
moments, seemingly taking refuge from the tension and delicacy of
the human confrontation by occupying himself with the mechanical.

The telephone is the mechanical link between the two houses,
just as the radio linked airport and houses. Geneviève agrees to
meet Robert the next morning, and the camera tracks with her as
she walks back to the next room to rejoin her card-playing guests.
The radio has concluded the interview and launches into the waltz
of an accordion band. The guests, a Homosexual and Saint-Aubin
(who is also in love with Christine) gossip about Christine and
André behind her back. Although they also know about Geneviève
and Robert ("Like everyone"), they do not gossip about that because one of the parties is present. The Homosexual (and several
of the other characters) seemingly spend all their time in the film
playing cards (belotte) and gossiping. Their attachment to cards
not only establishes the importance of games to them but also reduces the more serious social relationships to a game.

The scene concludes (the scene in Geneviève's apartment is a
single take, lasting almost a minute and a half, using both camera
movement and depth for variety) with Geneviève's cynical declaration: Love in society is merely a product of the imagination (a
meeting of two fantasies) and the body (a meeting of two skins).
Is that Renoir's definition of the game that causes the chaos and
catastrophe of this film? Is love no more valuable or serious than
a game of cards?

The second sequence of the act contains two scenes that are
more isolated than those of the first sequence, which were linked by
the radio broadcast that concerned all the characters. The scene
between Robert and Geneviève, in which he insists that he must
break off with her to be worthy of his wife, begins with a dissolve,
a punctuating device that Renoir does not use frequently in the film,

preferring instead the more conclusive break of the fade out. Renoir dissolves from Genevieve's deflation of love to her attempt to keep possession of Robert, whom she says she loves. Again Renoir uses the tracking shot and the movement of the characters to mirror emotional agitation in this delicate scene. Renoir positions the two figures at opposite sides of the room, providing another interesting visual perspective as well as implying the distance that Robert is trying to put between them.

The central device of the scene is that both Robert and Geneviève lean on statues of the Buddha—a traditional symbol of love, friendship, mildness, and order. As in his earlier telephone call to Geneviève, Robert instinctively feels the need to lean on some device of apparent order and stability. In this sense, the statue of Buddha parallels the music boxes around which Robert's world and feelings revolve. Indeed the Buddha seems to triumph over Robert's determination, for he is incapable of breaking with Geneviève and causing her pain. Robert confesses that he is a weak man. Ironically his weakness is a kind of strength, for it makes him incapable of deliberately hurting anyone. But mustn't his weakness eventually hurt someone if their private knowledge becomes public enough for Christine to find out about it? This contradiction—that Robert does not want to cause pain but cannot avoid causing it—is central both to his character and to the issues of the film.

The conversation ends as Robert walks toward Geneviève (and the camera tracks backwards), healing the distance that he attempted to put between them. The two go off to lunch, a perfectly acceptable, polite way to end a disagreeable discussion and a clear implication that Robert's relationship with Geneviève will continue—which it does. The scene ends with Robert's inspecting some gladioli, finding some defect in a flower, and tossing it away. Ironically, he is more successful at eliminating a defect in a floral arrangement than in a human one.

The second scene shows André so upset by Christine's rejection that he either inadvertently or intentionally smashes his car against an embankment. As with the airport scene, Renoir handles this nervous, excited event by keeping the moving camera on faces, supported by off-screen noise (of the racing engine). The crash itself occurs in a distant far-shot, so quickly and distantly photographed that the audience feels no real fear or suspense about the result (which would be inappropriate at this point in the film). Ironically, André is far more successful at flying across the Atlantic in an airplane, which is an extraordinary feat, than in driving an automobile, which is a very commonplace one. (A further unstated irony is that the accident takes place at the exact spot where Renoir himself was injured in a serious automobile accident, in which the driver, his friend Pierre Champagne, was killed. Renoir was rescued from his accident and taken to the hospital by poachers—a motif that also appears in *The Rules of the Game.*)

In the dialogue scene that follows the crash, Renoir succeeds admirably with a very difficult problem: how to convey an immense amount of information without the scene's becoming heavy-handed and dead. He does it in two ways. First, he chooses a deliberately strange camera angle, an awesome upward shot from a very low angle that emphasizes the speakers as two soaring heads against the magnificent sky. Second, Octave delivers his oration—that he is Christine's protector, that André is an idiot on the ground, that André violated the rules of Christine's world by confessing his love in public on the radio—with incredible rapidity and agitation. The agitation is motivated by Octave's recent scare, but the goal of the scene is to reduce the importance of the words by reducing speech to sound, to an aggressive noise. The noise even begins before the speaker enters the frame. The real communication in the scene is less verbal than physical, Octave's using speech as a kind of club or goad. But Octave, a mild and docile friend, cannot keep clubbing for long. He, like Robert, softens at the end of the scene. Indeed, the scene is a mirror-image of the preceding one: like Robert, Octave is a weak man who cannot stand to see anyone suffer. And so Octave agrees to help André, just as Robert agreed to take Geneviève to lunch.

The final sequence of the act is more complicated than the second, expanding the two previous duets to a quartet. Octave is the focal figure of the sequence, bringing Lisette, Christine, and Robert together, as well as playing duets with all three of them. The issue of the scene is getting both Christine and Robert to agree to invite André to La Colinière.

In the shots of Octave's entering la Chesnaye's house, Renoir again uses the tracking camera to mirror the movement of the characters. In addition to the activities of the principals, Renoir's deep shots of the corridor show the whole society of the house at its business. Octave's meeting with Lisette brings the two "servants" together for the first time—Lisette, who defines herself in terms of Madame, and Octave, who defines his life at this moment in terms of André. Octave's meeting with Robert then brings the two "weak" men together for the first time, and Robert shows Octave a new warbler that chirps every twenty seconds—another conversion of imperfect nature into perfect machine.

The quartet scene embracing all four of them centers around Lisette's husband, Schumacher, who wants his wife to live with him and not Madame. Robert takes the side of the film's other husband, urging Lisette, not without irony and humor, to return to him. She refuses to consider it; for her, as for Madame, marriage has its limits. Two other motifs emerge from the quartet. First, Robert pronounces Schumacher's name as Shoo-mah-SHAIR and Christine corrects that to SHOO-mah-ker. This contrast of French and German pronunciations both alludes to Christine's problem as an Austrian in a foreign society as well as reveals the internationalism of the Paris society. Further, Schumacher is Alsatian, a province that Germany and France had been fighting about for almost a century. The intrusion of Christine's German seems a subtle reference to the current European political situation in which Germany is threatening to intrude into all of European society and usurp it.

Second, Christine greets Octave with such warmth that she fails to notice her own husband. Robert must brush past Octave through the door (one of several shots that Renoir takes through doors in the film, and one of his favorite devices) to greet his own wife. Robert even emphasizes the awkwardness of his being excluded with a sharp "May I?" to Octave, a polite request that his voice coats heavily with irony. The slight, barely voiced tension between these two men foreshadows the ultimate revelation that Octave is Robert's most serious rival.

The scene between Octave and Christine further prepares for that revelation. After Christine finally relents in her banishment of André, despite her fears of impropriety, the two "friends" (is friendship with a man possible? Christine earlier asked) throw themselves down laughing on the bed. Christine lies on top of Octave (even here Octave plays the passive role) and the two chatter affectionately—lying in a sexually charged position and on a sexually associated object. In addition, the bedplay with Octave is one of Christine's first vibrant, natural, warm, and convincing moments in the film, the first sign of life she has shown. Octave, however, responds to her playfulness as pure play and merely feels relieved of his obligation to André. Octave's appetite returns, and for the second time in the film a scene of emotional tension ends with the desire to eat.

The scene between Octave and Robert begins with Robert on the telephone with Geneviève once again. For the first part of the scene between the two men, Renoir uses another of his interesting spatial compositions, arranging the speakers on the sofa facing each other in visually contrapuntal positions, so that the original shot (which favors Robert) and reverse shot (which favors Octave) seem to give entirely fresh and different perspectives on the conversation. This method is in sharp contrast to the American method (which Renoir deplored) of putting the two speakers in a single plane, practically facing the camera, so that the reverse shot merely gave the second speaker's reactions rather than an entirely different slant on their spatial relationship. The two men talk jokingly about marrying Geneviève off; Octave even offers to sacrifice himself, "servant" that he is. But when Octave proposes inviting André to La Colinière, Robert is troubled (despite having just invited his own mistress there).

And when Robert is troubled, he begins to walk. Renoir's camera moves with him in a magnificent 180° counter-clockwise tracking shot to mirror that trouble (in *The Crime of M. Lange* Renoir and Bachelet execute a full 360° tracking shot). When Octave begins to feel that his request might be rejected, he begins to wish that he could separate himself from people and their passions completely, for "everyone has their own good reasons." But what if one man's good reasons are bad reasons for another? And what if one man's good reasons conflict with another's? How can one produce order out of a chaos of "good reasons?" These complex implications springing from Octave's simple assertion are never explicitly or specifically explored in the film (as is typical of Renoir). Octave simply makes his statement and the subject then seems to be dropped. But those questions lurk behind the rest of the film's action and become, perhaps, its ultimate questions.

Robert seems to perceive the import of Octave's statement, for immediately after it Robert begins to fiddle with one of his mechanical gadgets, a gramophone. At the same time, he agrees to invite André, stating that his "good reason" is that he wants no barriers, no walls in his life (despite the barrier he has erected with Geneviève). As in the scene with Geneviève, Robert busies himself with a machine when the human passions and tensions about him verge on chaos (most strikingly with his huge mechanical organ at the party). And so often he seems to use the machine to overlook the fact that he is one of the causes of the chaos. A glimpse into the link between the orderly machines and the order Robert would like to establish in his life comes just after this scene with Octave. Robert loses the key to the warbler in his hallway, and he rather desperately and undecorously begins to search for it on his hands and knees.

Despite the brief scare over the loss of his key (which foreshadows his more serious scare about losing Christine at the end of the film), the act ends with gayety and apparent accord. Like the two scenes before it, early tension evaporates into relaxed agreement. Octave gets his breakfast and chases Lisette playfully around a table (later Marceau will chase Lisette lecherously around another table). Robert then humorously labels Octave a "dangerous poet." The charge might be levelled at the filmmaker playing the role (who makes dangerous and disturbing works of "poetry") as well as the character himself (who proves very dangerous to André when he "poetically" sacrifices himself for André's happiness). The act fades out with the bouncy singing of *Tra-la-la* from the phonograph.

ACT 2

The film's second act builds the individual human beings introduced in the first act into a total society. Or rather two societies —the society of masters and the society of servants that mirrors that of the masters. In taking the characters out of Paris and confining them to La Colinière, Renoir not only achieves the isolation required to examine an entire social microcosm but also transports the people of the twentieth century into the past, into an eighteenth-century chateau that allows them the pure aristocratic idleness of eighteenth-century life. Leisure becomes a mode of existence itself. These rich, aristocratic people of the world can retire from the pressures of that world into an artificial one of their own. This self-contained world, then, can also develop the terms in the film's title, for at La Colinière life is a pure and undiluted game, and its rules are equally pure and strict.

The act is structured around four arrivals, the introduction of four newcomers—Robert (who apparently has not visited La Colinière for some time); Geneviève (very much a part of the game, but a threat to the stability of Robert's life); André (who is so pure, passionate, and naïve that he is totally unsuited to play the game because he despises its rules); and Marceau (who is as much a stranger to the game as André, but who aspires to play it well).

Two automobiles carry Robert, Christine, Lisette, Corneille, and the other personal servants into the grounds of La Colinière. Ironically, they need the machines of the twentieth century to transport them back to the eighteenth. After perfunctory hellos and greetings—including a particularly clumsy and unemotional reunion between Lisette and Schumacher—the first major sequence takes place on Robert's grounds as he surveys his world. This is the first major outdoor sequence in the film (the airport sequence was so dim and tightly shot that it seemed claustrophobic and more like an indoor scene), and prepares the audience for the major outdoor sequence of the hunt in the next act. The look and texture of the outdoor shots are in marked contrast to those indoors—luminous and soft views of fields and trees, the leaves and branches delicately etched against the sky. Indeed, the juxtaposition of branch and sky is perhaps the most common natural image throughout Renoir's films. But in the outdoor sequence Renoir uses precisely the same camera strategy as in the indoor ones—tracking shots, pans, and composition in depth.

The ostensible subject of the outdoor sequence is rabbits. For the first scene, between Robert and Schumacher, Renoir uses a single take, a tracking shot, that lasts almost a full minute. The off-screen pop of rifles in the distance, which foreshadows the more brutal on-screen shooting in the next act, also brings Robert to a discussion of the rabbit problem with Schumacher. The rabbits, unimpressed by the boundaries and rules of men, insist on invading the grounds of the estate to do damage to the plants of the chateau. Rabbits, like Octave and Geneviève, like to eat. Schumacher suggests a fence to keep the rabbits away, but Robert does not want any fences. He also doesn't want any rabbits. This contradiction (about which Schumacher later grumbles with his men) that Robert wants neither rabbits nor fences is parallel to all the other contradictions of Robert's life and world—it cannot be both spontaneous and mechanical, honest and hypocritical at the same time. And yet that is precisely what Robert wants it to be.

The next scene, between Schumacher, his men, and Marceau, introduces living animals to the film. Unlike the controlled, disciplined actions of men, the rabbits scamper chaotically and miscellaneously about the grounds, pure beings of nature who care neither how nor where they are moving. There are two other animals in the scene—both domesticated. The dog, Musette, has become an ally of men; even her name reveals how much she is a part of their world. A cat, however, fares less well, trapped in one of the cages meant for the chaotic rabbits. Schumacher reveals his brutality by taking a shot either at the cat or just to frighten it away (the published script states that Schumacher shoots at the cat, but it runs off to Schumacher's left and he takes the shot to his right).

The discovery of a rabbit in a snare leads Schumacher to his first denunciation of Marceau. Ironically, Marceau, whom Schumacher considers an enemy, is really an ally. He is helping to clear the estate of rabbits. But he is not helping to clear it in the accepted way; he breaks the rules of rabbit clearing because he does not simply want to destroy rabbits but needs to eat them to survive (just as the rabbits need the chateau's plants to survive). Marceau is a poacher who, like the rabbits, invades the estate that belongs to someone else—even if his activities really help the man who owns that estate. Schumacher is as concerned about rules as anyone else in the film.

After his introduction, Marceau himself enters the estate, his movement captured by another tracking shot, muttering to himself (much as that other man of nature, Boudu, was introduced in his film, inarticulately muttering and grunting to himself). Marceau is the low-comic buffoon of traditional comedy. The actor who plays him, Julien Carette, specialized in playing clowns. But there is an unmistakable Chaplin quality about the role as well—the tramp, the man outside of society surviving on his instincts and resilience, intimidated by the respectable because of the way respectability defines him. The conflict between Marceau and Schumacher, on opposite sides of the rules of killing rabbits, resembles the antagonism between Chaplin and Eric Campbell in the Mutual shorts. And Renoir admits that Chaplin was one of the dominant influences on his films and imagination. Many of Marceau's shrugs, grimaces, and movements even resemble, if not Chaplin, then the entire American school of silent-film clowning. And the battles between Schumacher and Marceau—both their childish name calling and the gruesomely slapstick tug-of-war with the corpse of the rabbit—also resemble the clowning in American films (a Laurel and Hardy duel, for example) despite the serious edge to the farce.

Ironically, when Schumacher marches Marceau over to feel the wrath of the master (and again the camera marches with them), Robert realizes that Marceau is an ally despite the illegality of his methods. But when Robert offers Marceau a job working for him, the poacher does not poeticize the joys of nature and the outdoors. He would rather work indoors, not only to escape Schumacher's territory (Marceau later "poaches" on another piece of that territory) but because he has always dreamed of wearing the uniform of a house servant. Marceau is a man of nature merely out of necessity. He longs to play the same genteel game by the same artificial rules as everyone else. In Marceau's longing to be a domestic (*domestique*), Renoir's film begins to develop the linguistic parallels between "domestic" (meaning "servant") and "domesticate" (meaning "tamed," "civilized") as another of the metaphors that relate nature and society. The sequence ends as the shot (another of Renoir's magnificent low-angle shots emphasizing the faces of men against the sky) fades out, accompanied by Robert's laugh about the poacher who yearns to be respectable, a man of the wilds who longs for "domestication."

The arrival of Geneviève gives Renoir the opportunity to introduce the other house guests as well, beginning the depiction of the entire society that serves as the environment for the remainder of the film. Geneviève arrives in a driving rain storm; the rain, though one of the accidents of bad weather that Renoir faced on location, also mutes the atmosphere of the scene and is a foreshadowing of the more serious human storms to follow. The camera begins as outsider in the shot, following Geneviève as she leaves her car and enters the house, holding itself outside the doorway looking in at the group. The camera then moves inside to join the group in the next shot. We, like the camera, are now part of the society indoors.

Renoir's handling of talk and sound in the scene of greetings parallels his handling of Octave's lecture to André in the accident scene. Renoir moves the dialogue very quickly, deemphasizing individual words and speakers, increasing the general impression of energy, excitement, and conviviality. Renoir again reduces words to a tonal collage of sounds, an almost inarticulate human babble. The pace slows and the noise subsides for the final dialogue of the sequence—Geneviève's confidential exchange with Robert—which is private information intended for Robert's ears alone and not for the public social gathering.

Renoir uses Christine as the focus for André's arrival (Robert has so far served as the focal figure of the second act). The first part of the scene begins in the kitchen where Renoir introduces the film's second society. Two tracking shots reveal the activity of the kitchen at work, the special needs of some of the guests, and the fact that the servants are as aware of their masters' affairs as the society upstairs. Renoir uses a second shot through a doorway—this time from the inside looking out, the reverse of the shot introducing Geneviève—for André's arrival. Christine freezes slightly as she sees him—the brief take reveals either her anxiety or her relief about his coming. She recovers to tell Madame de la Bruyère who he is as Renoir's camera executes another semi-circular track to view the new arrivals from Christine's point-of-view.

Octave greets Christine and she first greets him rather than André. Christine, ironically, is the only one who greets Octave, all of the other guests taking interest in the hero rather than the friend. Christine greets André with icy politeness, but Robert's greeting of the man he fears as his rival is far more energetic—good form perhaps, but slightly over-eager and excessively animated at the same time, accompanied by Robert's bustling cross and his putting his arm around Christine's waist. Robert rather successfully asserts himself as host, friend, and husband at the same time. The greetings of the other guests are far more distinct and much slower paced than in the parallel scene with Geneviève. André is a more special guest and there is far more tension in his arrival. Saint-Aubin, the Homosexual, and Charlotte gossip about André and Christine in a quiet corner, but the General refuses to hear such talk and finds André a real man, one of a race which is disappearing from the earth. Ironically, one more member of that race will disappear in the course of the film.

Christine stops the talk and relieves the tension with her open admission to the entire group that she and André spent many hours together in "friendship." Renoir begins with her walking toward André in another tracking shot, and before her confession she startles the group by embracing him openly. But her voicing aloud the supposedly secret information that before had only been whispered converts the private issue into a public one and totally defuses it. One can no longer whisper quietly about matters which have been loudly proclaimed. Further, for Christine to proclaim the relationship aloud takes all the salaciousness out of it, for would she dare confess publicly to a relationship if it hadn't been harmless?

That question indeed lies behind Christine's confession, for the audience (and perhaps even some of the guests) cannot be quite certain of what Christine is saying beneath the words. Is the confession sincere or pretense, honest admission or merely a magnificently subtle ploy? Her recitation is so formal and stilted—perfectly fitting the formality of the social gathering perhaps—that it again seems divorced or not completely allied with whatever she might be feeling. As with so many of Christine's statements, her open admission is ambiguous and unclear both in its ultimate intent and its relationship to her internal feelings.

Robert's reaction is not unclear. He addresses his guests with great exuberance and expansive gestures. The tension of the previous scene completely relaxes and Renoir ends the encounter with the same fast-paced, almost indistinguishable babble of human voices that he used for the arrival of Geneviève. The obstacle that endangered the success and felicity of the social gathering has been surmounted. The social game can continue; the rules have not been broken. The general hum of social conviviality returns to the picture and sound track as the scene fades out.

Marceau's arrival, like André's, begins in the kitchen, which parallels them as interlopers. The society of servants is at dinner, and their society parallels the one upstairs. Corneille is the head of that society, the master of the servants just as Robert is at the head of the society upstairs. Although Corneille heads this society, he does not sit at the head of the table. Lisette, Madame's personal servant, sits there, occupying the position of second-in-command, just as Christine does upstairs.

The servants spend their time gossiping about the same matters as the masters upstairs. The servants are concerned about Christine's affair with André. Lisette must defend her mistress, not by denying the existence of a lover but by implying that any young, attractive woman has the right to have lovers. The servants are as aware of the rules of the game as anyone: "conventions are conventions." Any blot on the reputation of their employers seems a blot on themselves as well. The servants are also narrow-mindedly class conscious. A chauffeur makes a slur on Robert's Jewish origins (another sign of the political times), but the chef defends Robert's claim to aristocracy on the basis of Robert's aristocratic tastes in food. Robert is enough of a gourmet to know whether a potato salad has been properly prepared or not. Food defines the aristocrat for the chef, just as amorousness defines an aristocrat for an amorous maid, a good automobile defines an aristocrat for a chauffeur, and a good huntsman defines an aristocrat for a gamekeeper. The servants are ironically more conscious and more explicit about social propriety and conventions than the people upstairs who are living that propriety and those conventions.

Into this tightly regulated and controlled society enters the unconventional Marceau, just as the unconventional André entered the tightly regulated society upstairs in the previous scene. Marceau is shabbily dressed; he walks and speaks sloppily. The camera tracks with him as he tentatively enters this den of snobs. The clumsy outsider doesn't even have a domestic specialty. His belated recollection that his specialty is dressing seems particularly strange since he himself is dressed so shabbily. Marceau's being a stranger in such a group becomes especially clear when one of the servants sneers at the thought of eating rabbit, which is Marceau's means of survival.

Lisette alone finds the man attractive—because he is a man. And he finds her attractive as well, until he finds out that she is his hated enemy's wife. This convention in no way inhibits Lisette's flirtatiousness, and the poacher's natural lecherousness overcomes his fears and inhibitions as well. Renoir ends the sequence by transporting us from the world of the servants to the world of the masters by means of a dissolve—from the kitchen radio (playing the "Minute Waltz") to the ornate clock upstairs that measures the minutes and chimes the hour.

The hour is late; the final sequence of the act becomes the first of the film's three corridor scenes and the first of three scenes in which the hosts politely bid goodnight to their guests. For most of the sequence in the corridor Renoir uses a single take—the second longest one in the film, lasting about 100 seconds—that both tracks with the moving characters and reveals the extreme length and breadth of the imposing hall. The corridor is a kind of visual translation of the film's essential contrast between private emotions and the public face. The corridor contains two architectural features. It is itself a large public room where the inhabitants of all the rooms can mingle. And it presents a series of doors through which a character can step to be alone with his own thoughts, feelings, words, and deeds.

Renoir's hallway scenes use both the public and private regions, as well as emphasize the differences between the two. In the hallway, Robert and Christine bid goodnight to all the guests, a matter of politeness, propriety, and good social form. In the privacy of Christine's doorway, Robert thanks his wife for her skillful handling of a delicate situation with André. In the public corridor characters discuss such trivialities as the party, pre-Columbian art, card tricks, fencing ploys, and hunting horns. The childish clowning of the goodnight games in the hallway (pillow throwing, mock fencing) is a magnified parallel of the more elegant games played downstairs in the grand salon (as the party sequence makes quite clear). Inside the rooms, however, Christine discusses love and marriage with her maid Lisette and André confesses his misery.

Whereas Robert and Christine are the focal figures of the public part of the corridor scene, Octave is the focal figure of the private part. He plays individual scenes with Lisette (with whom he is energetic and aggressive), Geneviève (who is contented now that people are beginning to "play their cards"—more terms of games), the General (who, as always, is concerned about class and style, how well people play the game), and André (who wishes he had never come since the game is so foreign and painful). The act fades out with a few final flourishes of Berthelin's hunting horn on the sound track; the music introduces the hunting sequence in the act that immediately follows.

ACT 3

The business of the third act is the hunt, and that business is significantly different in both function and cinematic style from any other act. First, the hunt does almost nothing to advance the plot. Except for its final moments it is completely unrelated to what is by now clearly the story of the film; several interlocking love triangles (Geneviève–Robert–Christine–André, Schumacher–Lisette–Marceau) played against the background of two societies—that of the masters and of the servants. The third act is a kind of intermission, after which the main plot returns with full force and even greater complexity.

The function of the hunt scene is clearly thematic and metaphoric. The masters and servants have taken their games, normally played in the salon and the kitchen, into the natural domain of the outdoors. The elegant, formal, civilized aristocrats (and the servants who serve as their accomplices) have entered the chaotic world of the rabbits. The result of their brutal invasion is not a healthy game for the rabbits (and pheasants). If Robert's mechanical dolls and birds reveal him giving a kind of perfect, orderly, regulated life to that which is dead, the hunt scene does quite the reverse—robbing the vital birds and animals of the breath of life with the swift crack of another human machine, the rifle. Although the hunting scene is one of the shorter sequences in the film, it remains one of the film's most powerful and memorable sections, casting its emotional spell over the remainder of the action and obviously demanding consideration in any intellectual speculation about the film's ultimate statement and values.

The act is as different technically from the rest of the film as it is structurally. Renoir still uses tracking and panning shots, particularly of the tromping men and scurrying animals; as in the earlier outdoor scene on Robert's grounds, Renoir juxtaposes men and nature, human figures with the trees, fields, and sky. But the essential stylistic difference is Renoir's use of montage. The sequence relies on editing—cuts from the hunters to the prey, cuts from dying rabbits to dying pheasants, cuts from one scurrying, frightened rabbit to another. The cuts not only convey the information about the slaughter but also convey the rhythms and energy of the hunt itself. There is so much slaughter in so little time. The pace of the sequence is extremely rapid—death after death after death—in quick, rhythmic succession. The first five reels of the film average one cut approximately every thirty feet (every twenty seconds). The sixth reel (which contains the hunt as well as the introductory preparations of the hunters) averages one cut every ten feet (every seven seconds), giving the act a completely different rhythm and feeling from the rest of the film.

The different rhythm contributes, in turn, to the thematic function of the act, which is to depict brutal, senseless, and useless murder. Its tone differs strikingly from what both precedes and follows it, for here Renoir indulges consciously in both pathos and horror for the only time in the film. Whereas the other sections of the film maintain a polished, objective distance from the human figures—the film feels like a sophisticated, witty comedy of manners intent merely on skating along a hard, cold surface—this section shows great compassion for the suffering figures (who, ironically, are not human). Renoir conveys his compassion by watching the death agonies of the animals minutely and unflinchingly, instead of focusing on the hunters as he might have done.

The first section of the hunt transports us visually from the indoors to the outdoors. But the characters continue to devote themselves to the polite forms of the salon. La Bruyère and Saint-Aubin discuss a disputed pheasant with great politeness, each graciously and unselfishly offering the prize to the other. Each of the hunters takes his assigned and numbered position. Schumacher is like a theatre usher, showing the audience to its seats. This audience, however, is not going to watch but act, and the act it will perform after all the gentility and polish is murder. The masters stand in a long, precise line, another evocation of the symmetrical rows of theatre seats, ready for the prey. Visually the hunters form a human corridor that is as precisely symmetrical and regular as the corridor of the chateau with its bedroom doors.

Neither André nor Christine takes much interest in the hunt. André, true to his own passions and commitments, refuses to take part in the social game and merely complains to Octave about Christine. In the course of the hunt, we never see André take a single shot at an animal. Christine is equally true to herself. When Jackie, her niece, who loves André herself, asks her if she likes hunting, Christine makes a totally ambiguous series of facial expressions that say, successively, yes and no, or, rather, neither yes nor no. That series of uncommitted expressions is perhaps Christine's essential moment in the film, the one moment that defines her completely.

The beaters stand in a row (as regular and precisely formal as the hunters) and begin their march forward. If Schumacher is a theatre usher to the masters, he is a military general to the army of servants. The servants begin their march forward, beating the trees with sticks, an evocatively hollow sound that is parallel to the sound the masters make with their rifles. The terrified animals huddle in fear as the masters load their rifles (an effective use of cross-cutting by a director who is not noted for his cutting), and the rabbits and pheasants then scurry chaotically, frenziedly to escape. The series of shots that follows is the most difficult thing in the film to describe in words, for it is the least verbal section of the film.

The gruesome, pathetic, and horrifying effect of all the slaughter arises from our seeing the actual expiration of a living being before our eyes. A rabbit bounds across screen. The crack of a rifle suddenly halts the animal in the middle of its progress. Its legs stretch out and seem to stick together. Its body, completely out of the animal's control, flips over, and then stops. No movement at all. Motion has been converted to stasis. It is this essential element of *motion* pictures (the ability to differentiate between bodies in movement and at rest) that Renoir uses to depict the horrifying effect of death.

The death of the pheasants uses a different principle of *motion* pictures—the ability to differentiate between movement in different directions. The frightened birds take to the air. The rifle cracks and the bird is suddenly halted in its flight; its body leaves the horizontal plane and points itself toward the earth. It falls to earth in a pathetic nose dive, controlled by gravity and not by its own vital energy. As with the rabbits, the bullet robs the bird of its self-directed and self-controlled locomotion and brings it under the control of something outside itself—the earth. The dead animal is transformed into a clod of earth, and Renoir reveals that transformation from life to earth before our eyes.

The final death of the sequence is clearly its finale, an agonizing closeup of a rabbit who runs across the screen, flips over with its helpless legs in the air, and then with painful, infinite slowness stretches out to die. The blast of a hunting horn on the sound track signals that the dance is over—and a kind of cinematic dance of death it has been, the first of the film's "Danses macabres." But lest we take the hunt as the film's moral center as well as its structural center (it occurs in the middle of the middle act of the film's middle reel), we should first remember that Renoir himself had to kill a lot of rabbits in order to film the sequence (just as Jodorowsky had to do in *El Topo*). Renoir may be saying that hunting is merely a horrifyingly polite form of societal murder for the sake of entertainment, but he himself is doing precisely the same thing as the aristocrats in his film, for the sake of art. Before leaping to an easy conclusion about Renoir's moral criticism of the rules and the game it is worth seeing how he handles the film's remaining pieces.

The mood after the hunt is much less polite and more tense than before. In a beautiful Renoir long shot, which effectively uses filters to emphasize the heavy shapes of clouds that hang over the scene, we see the field littered with dead bodies; the obedient dogs (another set of servants) retrieve the game for the masters. La Bruyère and Saint-Aubin no longer argue graciously about a disputed pheasant, but openly accuse each other of trying to "poach" the bird for himself. Geneviève pulls Robert away from the group because she must speak to him "in secret"—a secret that everyone knows about. The General tells what he thinks is an amusing story of a man who blew his own leg off (and which is not very amusing, although Octave, the good mixer, forces himself to laugh at it). Jackie and André condole together, for she loves him and he loves someone else who apparently does not love him in return. And even the servants grumble about the incompetence of the hunters. A mood of mild disgust hangs over the whole party, just as the pendulous clouds hang in a dark sky over the darkening fields.

The central device in the final sequence of the act is Berthelin's field glass, another man-made device that improves on nature by helping the eye see better, further, more fully. Christine uses the machine to look at a squirrel, but Saint-Aubin's immediate reaction is to wish he had his gun. He can't seem to tolerate any animal's being left alive. But again Renoir balances the apparent brutality with Berthelin's reminder that squirrels (like rabbits) do a lot of damage. If one did not kill any rabbits or squirrels they would over-run the works of men, destroying the fields and crops that men had carefully cultivated. And Renoir seems to suggest that although the slaughter of animals is brutal, it is a necessary slaughter without which society and civilization cannot survive.

Eventually the field glass turns from the four-legged animals to two-legged ones when Christine accidentally catches Robert embracing Geneviève. Ironically, what she sees is their last embrace, Geneviève's realization that the relationship is over and Robert's responding compassionately (he is still a "weak" man) for the last time. This accidental discovery returns the film to its plot and propels the action into its concluding stages.

ENTR'ACTE

The next section of the film is not one of its major, extended acts but a bit of breathing space between the two major events of the hunt and the party. The entr'acte contains two short sequences— both of them essentially two-character scenes—that look backward toward what has preceded them and prepare the way for what is to follow. To preserve the film's analogy with the classical comic theatre on which it is modeled, the sequence resembles two brief dances that some of the play's characters perform in front of the curtain, before the author raises the curtain to plunge both us and the characters back into the world of the play itself. The two "dances" take us, alternately, to the domain of the masters (the corridor) and the domain of the servants (the kitchen), further emphasizing the parallels in those two regions as well as setting up the two separate strands of action that will be woven together in the next act.

The first scene reveals Christine's response to the embrace she witnessed in those field glasses. Under the pretext of a friendly, woman-to-woman chat (the interview's public face), Christine wants to find out exactly how deep Robert's relationship with Geneviève is (the private knowledge she wants to obtain). The scene is perhaps Christine's finest in the film, the one scene in which her external actions and her internal motivations are completely clear and harmonious. Ironically, Christine's words and actions are all lies in the scene—her friendliness, her apparently ingenuous smiles, her false confession that she has long known about the affair "like everyone," her ultimate strategy of discovering whether the two have slept together by referring to Robert's habit of smoking in bed. But at least in this scene Christine's words are transparent (to us, not to Geneviève) as lies, and her reasons for lying are clear.

When Christine changes the subject to talk about her own affairs—including her boredom with André and his sincerity—the old mysteriousness and vagueness return. Is this another strategic lie or the truth? (Indeed later events in the film support both contradictory possibilities). The scene between the two women ends with Christine's leaving the bedroom to return to the public world of the corridor, where the guests humorously wonder what has happened to their shoes. In the rapid convivial chatter the guests look forward to the celebration where Octave plans to dress as a bear—an appropriate costume for this bearish, lumbering man who has been "domesticated" by the society on which he is dependent for survival.

Clothing and costume serve as the link into the second sequence of the entr'acte. Schumacher gives Lisette her "costume" for the evening, the fatal cape, which will indeed disguise the identity of its eventual wearer far better than the other disguises. The cape also succinctly defines the differences between Schumacher and his wife.

The husband has bought it because it is practical; Lisette dislikes it because it is unattractive. The slight but obviously pained expression on Schumacher's face reveals that he is aware of the gap between his wife's values and his own, and that even his attempts to please her cannot succeed.

In the kitchen Marceau also occupies himself with articles of clothing, polishing the shoes that have disappeared from the corridor upstairs. Lisette's appearance in the kitchen interrupts his labors, and Marceau begins his flirtation, using one of Robert's mechanical dolls to tease and tempt her. As the doll's head moves (in another extreme close-up) and the apparatus emits its tinkling musical tones, Renoir again combines the cute and the grotesque, the attractive and the repulsively calcified evocations of such a machine. While the music plays and Marceau winks, Lisette coyly eats an apple (her first apple in the film), a second Eve tempting Adam to another fall. Renoir's use of the doll in the sequence seems to imply that the lecherousness-flirtatiousness of these two beings is as regular, as predictable, and as automatic as the activities of the doll. Although they are alive—and they are indeed exuberantly, vibrantly alive—there is something mechanical about their reactions to each other as well.

Marceau eventually takes the plunge—literally—by chasing Lisette around a table and then diving under it. Whereas Octave chased her around a table earlier, he never took that final plunge. And when Marceau seems to have hurt himself, Lisette drops her defenses and comforts him, and Marceau executes a typical Chaplin ploy to arouse sympathy as in such Mutual films as *The Fireman* (1916) and *The Pawnshop* (1916). But as Marceau and Lisette play their sexual games on the kitchen floor, Schumacher appears in the distant rearground, descending the stairs into the kitchen. This shot, one of Renoir's most effective uses of depth-of-field in the film, is brilliantly suspenseful, informing the audience of impending disaster for several seconds before Marceau and Lisette discover that doom is at hand. In the shot we first become consciously aware of the sound effect that accompanies Schumacher everywhere and becomes more and more attached to his ominous, fatal presence. The stiff leather of his highly polished hunter's boots squeaks menacingly whenever he takes a step.

Corneille enters to bring order to the kitchen; he will be less successful at controlling Schumacher in the next act. Schumacher warns Marceau that next time he will take a shot at him. Schumacher has talked of shooting so many times in the film that the audience can begin to believe him. As Shaw once observed, if a gun is introduced in the first act, it had better go off before the end of the play. In this film there has not only been a lot of talk about shooting, but guns have been going off since the beginning of the second act. Beneath the farcical, Chaplinesque antagonism between Marceau and the typical comic bully, there are foreshadowings of more ominous events.

ACT 4

The fourth act, the film's gala party of celebration, continues that tension between surface farce and ominous undercurrent. The act represents another huge shift in tone—from the most consciously brutal and pathetic third act to the most consciously comical and farcical one. More than any other section of the film, the party sequence feels and looks like classical farce, with various couples trying to duck off into a room alone, with various wronged suitors or husbands chasing after, with the chase of one suitor inadvertently revealing the whereabouts of a lover to another, and with all of the chases weaving inextricably in and out of each other. The act also features much slapstick material: two brawling fist fights so clumsy that they seem silly; a gun-shooting brawl that seems so ridiculous that the guests interpret it as merely one more item of entertainment on Robert's program. Indeed, Schumacher's antics with the pistol recall the gun-toting clowns in Mack Sennett comedies whom no one took seriously and whose bullets seemed no more lethal than a pie in the kisser. In *The Rules of the Game,* however, the Sennettesque bullets are indeed more lethal.

The dominant image of the fourth act is the theatre. As the characters perform acts on Robert's stage, other characters perform "acts" in the gun room, library, salon, and kitchen. The love chases of the various characters in the fourth act are very close to theatre, just as the film as a whole has consciously kept its eye on the conventions of the stage. When Octave asks Christine if she is going to act any more, she replies that she is tired of the drama. And when

Robert orders the usually unflappable Corneille to "stop this comedy," the fourth act has presented so many different comedies that the servant must ask, "Which one?" Perhaps the most theatrical event in the act is Octave's impersonation of Christine's famous father, standing on a stone balcony that converts him into a Greek tragedian in an ancient amphitheatre. And it is Octave who realizes the falseness of this truly tragic act.

In deliberately confusing the theatre and life, Renoir ironically comments on the difficulty of separating the two. While men costumed as skeletons perform a dance of death on Robert's stage, other men enact a real dance of death among the audience using real bullets. But whereas the theatrical dance causes the audience to scream with shivers of fear, the real death dance only arouses laughter and their suspicions of fakery. But Renoir's reduction of life into stage farce raises serious questions about the value and validity of the passions that his characters supposedly feel. Christine plays love scenes with no less than three leading men within a space of fifteen minutes. Which of those scenes (if any) is real and which are mere theatre?

In this act Renoir again returns to his use of the lengthy take, relying on camera movement and depth-of-field. This is an especially effective method for keeping the various chases together; nothing so specifically links the strands of action as one pursuer's disappearing in the rearground as another pursuer appears in the foreground or one couple's disappearing through a door in the rearground as another couple enters the frame in the foreground. Renoir's technique keeps both the action flowing and the disparate pieces convincingly tied together.

The camera technique is especially important to an act whose structure differs from that of any other. Whereas the other acts are composed of lengthy and developed scenes—each with a beginning, middle, and end—the scenes in the fourth act are brief confrontations, often interrupted before their conclusion by the appearance of another figure. Renoir also cuts away from a scene in progress, develops the beginnings of another, and then cuts back to the original scene for its conclusion. The moving camera and the use of screen depth link these disparate, often truncated scenes in both time and space.

The act begins at the public celebration where Robert and his friends perform on stage. The stage is, of course, a place where actors demonstrate their private emotions for a public audience. But Robert's stage—where the performers are also people with their private dramas—is different. Geneviève only flings her arms around Robert's neck when the curtain is closed. And Christine, witnessing this display, drags Saint-Aubin off the stage for some private scene in a more private place. Christine's sudden attraction to Saint-Aubin, whereas previously in the film she had scarcely seemed to notice his existence, is as mysterious as everything else she does in the film. Saint-Aubin has demonstrated his interest in Christine from his first appearance in Geneviève's apartment. But how long has Christine taken an interest in Saint-Aubin? Is her grabbing him away merely an act of spite or desperation?

Of all the acts on Robert's stage, perhaps that of André and Octave is the most pointed and ironic. André cracks his whip as Octave, in his bear skin, walks dutifully according to André's commands. In costume, as well as in life, Octave is the domesticated beast, never indulging his own tastes but merely obeying the dictates of others, particularly André's pursuit of Christine. This use of the play-within-a-film, in which characters perform actions on a stage that are closely related to their roles in the film itself, is a constant Renoir device—in *Grand Illusion* and, especially, in his late films, *The Golden Coach* and *French Cancan.*

The next theatrical item, the "Dance of Death," begins with a visual joke. Renoir begins the dance (as he began the act as a whole) with a shot of the piano keyboard. But this time the piano plays itself, a comically eerie touch for the eerie number to follow. In that dance (underscored by Saint-Saens' "Danse macabre") Renoir brilliantly captures the frightening, eerie quality of dancing skeletons (perhaps Disney's first Silly Symphony, *The Skeleton Dance* [1929], was an influence) by framing them with only the black drape, eliminating any reminder of the stage or audience, merely revealing a leaping white figure of death suspended in a black void. Renoir shows us the dance as the audience sees and feels it. No wonder they scream.

But there is another act taking place in the audience. In the flicker of the skeletons' lanterns we see Marceau embracing Lisette

—and Schumacher searching for his wife. We see Christine sitting quietly in a corner with Saint-Aubin—and André quietly observing Christine's infidelity. With this sequence Renoir deliberately scrambles and complicates the parallels that he has previously established among the characters. Whereas André previously paralleled Marceau, the poacher, in this sequence he parallels Schumacher (and later, Robert), the husband.

Unlike the other characters, Octave is not chasing after anyone else. He is merely trying to find someone to help him take off his bulky costume. But whereas Octave defines his life in terms of assisting others, he is unable to find anyone to assist him. He wanders from couple to couple and room to room, linking all the lovers and pursuers, ineffectually trying to remove the covering that restricts and degrades him. Indeed, the whole film might be seen as Octave's seeking to remove the clumsiness and cowardice that keep him from being a man. When Octave finally does get someone to help him with the bearskin—Geneviève—her efforts send him sprawling on the floor. Octave seems doomed to play the slapstick clown.

The sequence is built around corridors, rooms, and doors. Christine and Saint-Aubin flee into the gun room; Robert and Geneviève into the dining room. The two rooms are ironically next to one another—as Octave reveals when he goes from one couple to the other for help with his bearskin (and Renoir's shot-in-depth reveals Christine and Saint-Aubin through the open door). This technique of parcelling conflicting figures into separate rooms is a standard method of farce, descending from the two "houses" of Roman comedy (for example, Ben Jonson's *The Alchemist* or Feydeau's *A Flea in her Ear*). It is a standard Renoir method as well. In *Boudu sauvé des eaux* Boudu embraces Mrs. Lestingois in one room while Mr. Lestingois embraces the maid in the one next to it.

Marceau, however, does not use a door for protection but people. In the course of the act he hides behind Robert, Octave, Lisette, and Charlotte, Marceau's use of Robert gives the film's parallels another scramble. In this intimate scene (Renoir increases the intimacy by shooting it with a single take—the longest in the film), the gap between master and poacher shrinks. Both are men;

both are having troubles with women; neither wants to hurt anyone. Robert hates to make people suffer and Marceau likes to make them laugh. Despite Robert's love of the mechanical and perfect order, he, like Marceau, is capable of warmth, compassion, spontaneity, and humor. By this point in the film it is clear that Renoir's intention is not to establish simple categories—husbands and poachers, masters and servants—but to show that at times a husband can be a poacher, a poacher a husband, a master a servant and a servant a master. Renoir's view of human passions and aspirations is too complex to confine any character to a single category or definition.

Eventually the doors between the rooms must open, and Schumacher, one pursuer, serves as the accidental force that flings open the first door for another. He reveals Christine and Saint-Aubin embracing in the gun room, and his blundering response, "Oh, pardon," seems more like "oops." In the scene in the gun room that follows, André refuses to observe the social amenities, whereas both Christine and Saint-Aubin attempt to reassert the rules of certain games. André demands to know what Christine is doing and bashes Saint-Aubin in the face. Christine responds that André lacks tact and Saint-Aubin prefers a genteel duel with pistols. The rules are powerless, however, against a man who refuses to accept them, and the raucous fist fight is the result.

In contrast to the typical fist fights in American films, with each combatant delivering perfectly timed, sharp, almost balletic punches and parries, the fight in *The Rules of the Game* is a sloppy farce, with each pugilist attempting to deliver any kind of slap, kick, or punch possible. The farcical brawl is probably much more like a real fight than the heroic hand duels of Hollywood. The two fighters eventually spill out of the gun room and into the hallway, transporting their duel from the private to the public area. Corneille, the master of order in those public spaces, is there as always to pick up the pieces—both that of the fallen gladiator and the fallen Jackie who fainted during the fight.

André pulls Christine out of the public region and into the private one once again, closing the door of the gun room. And there Christine confesses that she really loves André. Is this the truth? Then why was she with Saint-Aubin? Why did she tell Geneviève she thought André a bore? Why has she shown no affection for

André throughout the film? Renoir increases the mystery of Christine's admission by using a far shot, not allowing us to get close enough to see what her eyes, her body or even her neck muscles might be saying beneath the words. Are they saying anything? Is Renoir deliberately making Christine a mystery or is he deliberately keeping the camera away from her to hide an inadequate performance? He gives André, not Christine, the close-ups in the scene.

André's response to Christine's confession is precisely the reverse of his attitude in his brawl with Saint-Aubin. Whereas Christine advocates the romantic, improper, asocial course of action —to leave the chateau together immediately—André suddenly becomes conscious of social form and the rules of the game. He cannot simply rob his host of his wife without an explanation. Why has André suddenly become a convert to the very rules he has despised? Does he now feel he is master of the game so he can afford to play it? Was his previous romantic naïveté a mere pretense? Once again, Renoir reveals that human actions are neither consistent nor schematic. Ironically, André's polite decision not to flee immediately is one of the causes of his death, an irony emphasized by the shots of the gun racks in the background of this scene.

At the climactic private moment when his wife is about to be "poached," Robert's public obligations also reach their climax. Rather than pursue Christine, he must demonstrate the culmination of his efforts as a collector of mechanical music boxes. The huge mechanical organ is indeed a culmination—in size, grandeur, and complexity. Can such an acquisition compensate for the loss of his wife? The answer to this question is complex and ambiguous, and the organ itself summarizes that ambiguity. The figure of a semi-nude woman is painted on the organ (Renoir shoots it in close-up), surrounded by electric lightbulbs. The painting appears flat and tawdry, especially emphasized by the electric lights and the machine's harsh music. This painted figure, however, is a typical ideal of romance and womanhood, a popularized, purified bastardization of a Rubens nude. Is Christine, the film's ideal of romance and womanhood, any more real, any less faded than the woman of paint? The painted woman is obviously dead. Is Christine any more alive? Or is the ideal of romance simply where men see it?

The camera explores further details of the organ that raise similar questions about Robert, its owner. In a single tracking shot, Renoir captures four figures, all in a single plane. The camera roams over one mechanical figure, then the second, then the third, and then, without breaking its rhythm or shifting its angle, comes to rest on Robert's face. The shot seems rather deliberately to have paralleled the living Robert with the three dead figures on his machine. Although Robert's responses to the success of this machine are quite complex—a mixture of pride, excitement, modesty, feverishness—is the man of flesh any more alive, any more free, any more flexible than the men of wood? Renoir's tracking shot implies that there is at least a sense in which Robert is as mechanical as his toys.

Robert demonstrates the sense in which he is more spontaneous and chaotic than the machine, however, in the next sequence, which draws him back into the slapstick farce by means of his servants. Marceau and Lisette take refuge once more in the kitchen (she again bites into an apple) when the squeaking leather of Schumacher's boots sends Marceau into hiding. Lisette tries to lie Marceau out of danger and her husband out of the kitchen with a series of romantic pictures of the natural beauties of Alsace. Marceau shatters the pretty lies with the crash of a tray, and the Sennett chase erupts again, out of the kitchen and into the hall upstairs—another private argument bursting into public. Robert orders Schumacher to stop, but the enraged husband is now so out of control that no social rules can control his fury—not even the master himself. The Sennettesque chase bursts into the gun room, interrupting André's idealistic and honorable sentiments in his conversation with Christine. Once again frenetic physical action pops the balloon of pretty words. First Marceau, then Schumacher, then Lisette dash past André and Christine, each stopping briefly (again in the Sennett manner) to make comic gestures of explanation before dashing off again.

The chase brings Robert into the gun room as well, just as Schumacher brought André there earlier. This time Robert finds himself precisely in the same position that André found himself earlier. And his reaction is identical. Whereas André now makes the polite gesture of good form, Robert violates form completely by punching André. The second brawl begins, making a shambles out of both the rules and the game, symbolized by the use of a huge shelf of books, those testaments to intellect, reason, and culture, as physical weapons in the brawl. Christine flees for the third time—this time with Octave.

The farcical chases and brawls culminate in an acceleration of both noise and pace. The first gunshot halts Robert's and André's fist fight. This is the first time a gun is fired at a human being in the film, and appropriately it occurs in the gun room. Renoir increases the frenzy with Geneviève's screaming hysterics and Robert's equally frenzied screaming in response. The rules and the game have disappeared, to be replaced by raw, uncontrolled human passion.

But in the midst of this frantic chaos, Renoir leaps to an oasis of quiet in Octave's scenes with Christine. This quiet will carry the film forward into the mood of its final act. The scene between Octave and Christine reveals a character who, for the first time in the film, is both self-conscious and aware of what he is doing. Octave neither blindly follows his own passions nor blindly follows the rules of propriety and good form. Octave is painfully aware that the activity on the surface of his life in no way compensates for the underlying emptiness.

Octave's impersonation of Christine's father is a piece of psychodrama, of his ambitions theatricalized into a stage show. Renoir's far shot turns Octave's projections into a kind of reality—a small, lighted human figure in the midst of a dark, vast stage, the orchestra of his dreams that he longs to conduct. But the shot also emphasizes the fact that the musicians are merely stones—the steps of someone else's chateau. Octave raises his hands in the gesture of a conductor, and on the sound track the music from a piano inside the chateau becomes suddenly noticeable. The music from the piano grows louder. The swelling music is a precise mirror of Octave's subjective perception—the swelling realization that he has no orchestra, only the music from someone else's party in someone else's chateau. Octave drops his hands. And with that simple physical act, Renoir communicates (both as actor and director) the complete emptiness that Octave so forcefully perceives. Octave sits down—another simple physical act that implies so much more than it states.

Renoir does not dwell on the quiet pathos at this point but cuts back to the climax of the farce inside the house. Marceau disguises himself by posing as a waiter with a tray (another Chaplinesque ploy). Lisette struggles with her husband for possession of the pistol and, accompanied by the music on the sound track, the two appear to dance a very bizarre waltz that is really a matter of life and death. In the rearground of Renoir's deep shot, we see Robert and André trying to manage the screaming Geneviève. Also in the rear of the shot, we can see two of Robert's stuffed pheasants lying askew on the floor of the gun room, a rather ironic contrast with the living pheasants that the hunters brought to earth in the hunt scene. In the drawing room the guests instinctively raise their hands at the sight of Schumacher's pistol, no longer quite sure whether they are participating in reality or a game. An effective Renoir tracking shot of their puzzled faces and rising hands mirrors their indecision and also adds a wry comic view of how these bizarre proceedings look to the outsiders who do not understand it.

Robert's mechanical organ, which has been accompanying the farce with its jolly music, suddenly goes berserk when Berthelin scrambles the mechanism in an attempt to turn if off. The climactic noises of the organ accompany the climax of the noisy, farcical act. The breakdown of the organ parallels the breakdown of the society, and the game, and the rules when confronted with the untamable chaos of genuine and irrational human passions. Corneille, as usual, brings the world back to order by deftly tripping up Schumacher and disarming him. The farce and the chaos come to a sudden halt.

ACT 5

The final act is a return to quiet and to order, but not the quiet or order that the characters expected. It is the quiet and order of death, and the entire act is shrouded in darkness and shadow to intensify that mood. Rather than beginning with a fade in that signifies a break in time, like the film's other acts, the final act continues immediately from the point at which the previous one ended. Rather than a break in time, the act begins with yet another leap in tone—from the most raucous, farcical act to the most somber and quiet one. The characters try to put back together the human pieces that have been shattered by the events of the party.

Eventually those pieces do fit together, but not in the way that anyone expected.

Whereas the fourth act was essentially a public one in which the various characters streamed in and out of each other's scenes, the final act is a series of small, two-character scenes in which the figures deliberately isolate themselves from the group to try to work things out between them. Ironically, one of the isolated couples mistakes the identity of another pair attempting to isolate themselves, and that mistake is the cause of the catastrophe. Whereas the previous acts juxtapose private passions with the public background of the society as a whole (and the fourth act was the culmination of this juxtaposition), the fifth act shows private passions working themselves out in private, with the public background returning only when an action occurs that requires a public explanation.

The act begins with putting the public society to bed—first the drunken Geneviève and fainting Jackie, then the rest of the supporting players. In this third corridor scene, the characters again withdraw from the public world of the corridor to the private one of their rooms, just as the act itself makes a similar withdrawal. This is the second of the film's "good night" sequences, in which the host politely ends the day's social life with the appropriate social amenities. But in this "good night" sequence, Christine is not present—as she was in the first series of good nights and as she will be at the final one. Octave is also missing, and his presence was especially pervasive in the first series of good nights in the corridor; he tied together the occupants of so many of the rooms. Although all the guests notice Christine's absence, no one misses Octave. Robert must then dispose of the two warring servants—dismissing both Schumacher and Marceau—before he can restore the peace and return to his conversation with André. The chaotic pieces seem to be falling together once again. The disruptive elements have been purged. The society and its rules reassert themselves as order returns to the chateau.

This order is especially clear in Robert's new attitude toward André, which has changed completely since the brawl that was interrupted by Schumacher's pistol. Good form and elegant grace have returned to Robert's manner; he apologizes to André for behaving so ungraciously. And André is so conscious of good form that he wears his dinner jacket. Robert now sees his burst of asocial passion as something completely foreign to himself, as the act of a stranger. He is incapable of understanding the crude, raw feelings of "peasants" who could kill each other for love. Of course, Robert himself displayed those very emotions near that very room not fifteen minutes earlier. Robert personifies the film's tension between passion and reason, chaos and order, self and society, spontaneity and form. And in his own inability to synthesize the two—both urges remain separate, alternating with one another—he also perhaps personifies Renoir's view of the essential tragic basis of the human condition.

But although order and reason return to the inside of the chateau, they do not return to the outside. The outdoors remains an area of nature and freedom, if also of chaos and savagery. The contrast of the film's third act—applying the laws of the salon to the grounds outdoors—reasserts itself in the final act of the film. Renoir reintroduces us to the outdoors with a tracking shot—first a statue (a sign of artifice and civilization), then a moat (the combination of the natural element of water with the artifice of architecture), but in the background are the untamed croaks of frogs and cries of birds. Outdoors it is dark, shadowy, frightening, whereas indoors it is light (although the lights are being extinguished in this act). Outdoors the irrational passions still reign. Octave and Christine can impulsively agree to run off together; Schumacher can impulsively shoot the man whom he thinks is stealing his wife. Christine seems to realize the difference between the two regions, for she believes she will never enter the chateau again. And when Octave does return there, the voice of reason returns to convince him that his actions outdoors with Christine were foolish.

The issue of Christine's first scene with Octave in the act is her discarding the artifice of her life inside the chateau. She discovers that even her closest friends—her maid and her brotherly protector —both knew about Robert's affair with Geneviève and hid the fact from her out of compassion and politeness. Of course they wanted to spare Christine's feelings, but, in addition, the stability of her entire life, her household, her social position were dependent on the preservation of social peace and the maintenance of the appearance of fidelity. To Christine's moral objection that such stability was a lie, Octave rebuts with his defense of lying. Everyone lies—governments, the radio, the cinema (a neat irony in which Renoir seems to warn us about taking his own film as anything but fiction).

Octave's defense of lying may well seem like an attack on society's hypocrisy and dishonesty. And to an extent it is. But lying seems one of those ingredients that also makes society possible. When men refuse to lie they race after each other with pistols. Although that kind of action is certainly more sincere, it is also more dangerous (as the film's conclusion makes quite clear). André is not murdered by a hypocrite but by a sincere man passionately acting out his own honest feelings. If all men were to act out their own passions there would simply be no society left. There would be no rules and no game—and no civilization. There would be no difference between men and rabbits. Perhaps the only real difference between men and rabbits for Renoir is that men are capable of building societies—which means they are capable of lying. With such implications arising from Octave's speech (and Octave is one of the most sympathetic figures in the film), Renoir's view of the tension between lies and sincerity, society and nature has become very cloudy indeed. The questions and contradictions are more obvious than any answer.

Christine also seems to perceive the implications of Octave's speech. In another of her beautifully perfect moments in the film, she throws back her head, opens her mouth, and seems to gasp for breath. In that gasp for clarity and purity there also seems to be a kind of sigh—the regret that lies are indeed an unfortunate human necessity. The scene ends with Lisette's draping the fatal cloak around Christine's shoulders.

The outdoors also provides a meeting ground for two men who were formerly enemies—Marceau and Schumacher. Indeed there is much about the men that ought to make them natural allies. Both are men of feeling; both are men of the outdoors. Schumacher's place is in the fields; he gets into trouble every time he enters the chateau. Marceau's place is also in the fields, although he would like to think of himself as belonging inside the chateau. But he is obviously out of place in the kitchen, just as his spontaneous and undiluted lecherousness has no place there either. Indeed, Schumacher's contempt for Marceau from the beginning has solely been based on the laws of the world of the chateau. Marceau's poaching is on the wrong side of the law from Schumacher's gamekeeping, but except for the law the two men do exactly the same thing. Marceau himself seems to realize this social fact, for he plans not only to return to poaching but to do so with a license. In the same way, isn't the difference between marriage and "poaching" a woman merely a matter of a license?

Renoir's camera remains outdoors for the next scene, Octave's (and perhaps Renoir's own) most self-conscious scene in the film. The man feels himself a complete failure and parasite; the artistic dreams of his youth have passed him by. He never made contact with the public; he can only make contact with the water with his spit. This scene between Octave and Christine is one of the quietest, the tenderest, and the most richly human in the film. Christine, as in her earlier scene with Octave in her bedroom, seems to come most alive in the scene. And Renoir tones the scene with darkness and shadow, which both enhances the softness and sincerity of Christine's responses as well as wrapping her face in darkness to increase the sense of mystery and distance about her. The shadows also make likely the mistake that follows, of Schumacher's mistaking Christine for Lisette.

Renoir uses another moving camera shot to link the two pairs of people outdoors. Renoir pans from Christine and Octave to Schumacher, linking the two in space. The shot-in-depth that follows allows both outdoor couples to share the frame at the same time— Marceau and Schumacher in the bushes, Christine and Octave in the greenhouse.

The greenhouse is an appropriate place for the climactic love scene between these two new–old lover–friends. A greenhouse is a man-made edifice designed to aid and improve nature. Its glass, an artificial product made from raw natural material, permits the flowers to obtain the beneficial light of the sun without exposing them to the harmful cold of the wind and frost.

Sheltered by the greenhouse, Christine can tell Octave that it is he whom she really loves. But is this remark to be taken at face value? Especially since Christine's face is again shrouded in darkness. Is this declaration of love more sincere than her declaration to André in the gun room? Or is it true that Christine loves best he whom she loves last? Christine's feelings remain shrouded—quite literally. The dark shot also provides a precise subjective translation of the way Schumacher sees the scene, how the distance and the darkness and the hood of the cloak mask the identity of the lady playing the love scene. But Octave, like André earlier, does not flee immediately with Christine but returns first to Robert's world. And that return, like André's, proves disastrous.

Inside the chateau the two former enemies, Robert and André, are as firmly linked as Marceau and Schumacher outside the chateau. But Robert and André, now operating under the assumptions of the indoors, see nothing to fear in Christine's being with Octave. Robert's belief in Octave's generosity and friendship is ignorant of the natural power of the outdoors. But when Octave returns from the outdoors to the chateau he also loses contact with the passion that he earlier felt.

Renoir builds the entire scene around Octave's searching for his battered, irrelevant hat. In a manner that closely parallels the last act of Chekhov's *Cherry Orchard,* a character blunderingly occupies himself with a trivial piece of clothing at what should be the climactic emotional moment of his life. Given Octave's preoccupation with the insignificant, he is now vulnerable to Lisette's arguments, who voices all the objections that a reasonable, nonpassionate person might make to the match—Octave is not attractive, he is not rich, and Christine could never be happy with him. Lisette's arguments are not disinterested ones, however. She is fighting to preserve her own life, of which Christine is the center and Robert's house the circumference. Her final plea, "Why not take me with you?" shows the real basis of her argument.

Lisette's reasons and the sudden return to the cold reasonableness of life inside the chateau weaken Octave's resolve. When André fires his question at Octave, "Where is Christine?" Octave faces a terrible dilemma—being false to his friend or false to himself. Inside the chateau Octave is incapable of being false to his friend. Renoir suddenly slows the pace, holding the camera on Octave's face as he pauses, reflects, then decides. He gives Christine to André—as he has done throughout the film—and he gives André his coat as well, the second piece of fatal clothing. As André rushes off to what he assumes is his joy, Octave takes off the hat that he has spent the entire scene trying to find and throws it to the ground in a gesture that combines disappointment, anger with the way things have worked out, and anger with himself for his own weakness. Robert and Octave now unite as the pair of mutual sufferers, replacing the male pair that opened the scene.

A tracking shot returns us to the outdoor world, linking Christine, Marceau, and Schumacher in the same fatal space. Because "Lisette" is now alone, Schumacher moves in to try to speak to her, an act that would have revealed his error and negated the tragedy to come. That tragedy, however, speeds toward them as, in a long, very dimly lit shot, Schumacher sees what appears to be Octave and immediately fires. André pitches forward in a small shaft of light, clasping his stomach, his two legs seemingly stitched together as they fling themselves uncontrollably into the air and then fall to earth. André's legs in death behave precisely like the rabbits' in the hunt scene. Marceau emphasizes the parallel in the next scene when he tells Octave that André took the shot like a rabbit.

But there is also a major difference in the death of André. André's death is far less pathetic, less touching, less sickening than the death of the rabbits in the hunting sequence. Rather than show André's death in close-up (as he does the rabbits'), Renoir's camera remains very far away. The scene is so dark and distant that André is only a falling figure. Renoir never allows us to see André's face, or body, or death agonies in close-up. We never see the body after it falls, unlike the corpses of the lifeless rabbits on the earth or in the dogs' mouths.

Renoir makes the death of André completely impersonal and emotionless. Since he made the death of a rabbit so pathetic he certainly could have done the same with the death of a man. Renoir drains the tragic deed of its pathos because he wants to emphasize not the horror of a man's death but the total process and pattern that has caused the death. Renoir's interest is the cause not the effect. Throughout the film, André, potentially a very compelling and sympathetic figure, has been kept at a kind of distance. Despite his heroism, his sincerity, his passion, and his uncorrupted naïveté, André never attracts us as much as Robert, Octave, Marceau, or Lisette. The actor playing the role, Roland Toutain, seems neither very sympathetic nor very attractive. The coldness and distance of his performance function much more clearly than that of Nora Grégor in the film, for André serves simply as the film's victim, the man who is expendable. If we cared too much about him, Renoir would lose his focus on why André must be the victim and why he is expendable. The impersonal death of André is consistent with Renoir's impersonal handling of this potentially romantic hero throughout the film.

Marceau and Schumacher both recognize their mistake immediately, and Marceau races to bring the news of the outdoor chaos to the people indoors. Ironically, Octave and Robert receive the terrible news as they sit in front of Robert's magnificent mechanical organ; that instrument of mechanical perfection will begin to reassert itself in the film's conclusion. Lisette, the servant who belongs in the mechanically perfect world, bids farewell to the two "servants" who do not belong. She and Corneille rush off to help the masters who need them. The two "poachers," Marceau and Octave, play their only scene together. Neither any longer has any business in Robert's house. Marceau has lost Lisette and his one chance for a respectable job. Octave has lost both André and Christine. Unlike Lisette and Corneille, they are no longer needed. Marceau goes off to poach in the woods, Octave to "poach" in Paris.

It may seem that Renoir himself is using the opportunity to turn his back on the dead values of Robert's mechanical world. But such a romantic supposition is probably unwarranted. Marceau, despite his alliance with nature and the outdoors, still envies Robert's world and is defined as an outsider and poacher only by its definitions. Octave is going to sponge off somebody else, for what else is he equipped to do? Although Marceau and Octave turn their backs on the chateau, it is the chateau that has triumphed.

That triumph is clear in the film's final scene which is—both physically and metaphorically—a return to the chateau. The characters all walk back toward the house, accompanied by the Mozart that has also returned to the film. Schumacher, previously dismissed for his murderousness, has now returned to the master's service because of it. His squeaking boots also accompany the procession, on the path and up the steps. Jackie, the passionate romantic who loved André, weeps and has her usual difficulties in remaining on her feet. Christine, however, has so mastered her feelings that she is a pillar of strength and an apparent mask of indifference. She mounts the steps to the chateau, the same steps where Octave earlier confessed his emptiness to her, and delivers the film's third polite wishes of good night to her guests. This time both host and hostess are present. The tension that earlier threatened the chateau, the marriage, and the game has been eliminated.

Robert turns to his "audience," standing on the same steps where Octave earlier played his theatrical impersonation, to play another theatrical scene. His "line" is that there has been a "regrettable accident," that his "keeper Schumacher thought he saw a poacher and fired," as was "his duty." (The film's English subtitles are woefully inadequate with this speech.) The ironies of this speech are richly related to the film as a whole. Of course Schumacher's action was not accidental but intentional. Further, Schumacher was no longer Robert's "keeper," having been dismissed after the party. And Schumacher knew that "Octave" was no poacher. But in another sense, he thought Octave was a kind of "poacher" who was about to bag his wife. Still further, it was not Schumacher's "duty" to shoot poachers since Robert himself realized that poachers did no damage but, quite the reverse, helped rid the grounds of rabbits.

Robert's speech is a complete tissue of lies—thicker and more complicated than even he realizes. The petty gossiper, Saint-Aubin, recognizes the lies, but the General, who has always respected style above content, finds Robert's lies a rare sign of class. In Renoir's view, however, the lies are not simply vicious nor admirable; they are inevitable, as inevitable as André's meeting Schumacher's bullet. What else could Robert do with the fact of André's death? Turning Marceau and Schumacher over to the authorities would serve no useful purpose (the murderer seems particularly guiltless in our eyes). This is a death for which everyone and no one is responsible. Robert himself reveals this tension and realization. In the close-up of his face we see tears in his eyes, affectingly genuine tears, at the same time that his mouth utters those ridiculously necessary lies. The tension between feeling and reason, passion and word that has controlled the entire film asserts itself forcefully in its climax.

The characters all return inside to the protection of the chateau —the protection it offers from the cold night air, from the chaos of unruled and unruly passion, and from the law of the state that will accept the lies of the chateau's owners as truth because it must. The final shot of the film is of the chateau itself, in a sense its triumphant character, as the Mozart on the sound track (and the graceful Mozart is the perfect musical ally of the world of the chateau) swells to its final chords.

summary critique

THE IMPLICATIONS OF A TRAGIC FARCE

The Rules of the Game is one of those rare works of film art that combines comedy and tragedy, murder and farce—combines them so successfully that the film feels neither funny nor pathetic but something between the two that differs from both. Renoir's control of tone in the film is such that he can leap from genteel objectivity to brutal pathos to ludicrous slapstick from act to act and scene to scene, without allowing any mood to nullify the others and without allowing any of them to seem out of place. Most of Renoir's films are either serious dramas (or even melodramas), like *Toni, Madame Bovary, The Lower Depths, Grand Illusion, The Southerner, The Woman on the Beach, The River,* or pure comedies, like *Boudu sauvé des eaux, The Golden Coach,* or *Picnic on the Grass.* In only a few of his films does he combine the tone, characters, and physical clowning of comedy with the serious act of death—*The Crime of M. Lange, The Elusive Corporal. The Rules of the Game* is Renoir's most successful (because it is the most inextricable) of these blends.

The amalgamation of comedy and death (theoretically the province of tragedy alone) is one of the major innovations of the twentieth century—in fiction (for example, Ford Maddox Ford's *The Good Soldier,* William Faulkner's *As I Lay Dying,* Joseph Heller's *Catch-22,* the short stories of Flannery O'Connor), in the drama (for example, most of the plays of Samuel Beckett, Eugene Ionesco, and Harold Pinter), and in films as well. But many of the films related to (or even descended from) Renoir's serio-comic blend tend to break into serious sections and silly sections more easily than *The Rules of the Game.*

Chaplin's *Monsieur Verdoux,* for instance, is a murderous farce in which the spirit of farce dominates most of the scenes; Chaplin interrupts the farce periodically to wax serious, after which he

returns to farce. Max Ophuls' *The Earrings of Madame de . . .*
(and Ophuls was heavily influenced by Renoir) begins as a comic
and ironic look at a superficial and materialistic society only to end
as a romantic melodrama. Ingmar Bergman's *Smiles of a Summer
Night* echoes the Renoir film in its genteel social milieu, its theme
of love and marriage, and its interweaving of several levels of action
and several social classes. But in the Bergman film death never
intrudes, although its shadow is evident. It is a film of light—both
visually and thematically—not of darkness. The threat of death
remains a farcical and theatrical stunt in the film—like the fourth
act of *The Rules of the Game* without the catastrophic final one.

Of all the contemporary directors, Stanley Kubrick seems to
have been most influenced by Renoir; the social elegance and
moving-camera technique of *Paths of Glory* (1957) seem to have
jumped directly off the screen of *Grand Illusion* and *The Rules of
the Game*. *Doctor Strangelove* is Kubrick's most obvious murderous
farce, but the satire and political burlesque in the film keeps its
tonal emphasis on farce. In *2001: A Space Odyssey* and *A Clockwork Orange* Kubrick interweaves the comic and the serious more
subtly, but both films are more distant and even tempered, never
reaching the pathetic depths and farcical peaks of *The Rules of
the Game*.

Perhaps closest to Renoir's tonal combination of gloom and
comedy is a predecessor rather than a descendant. Erich von
Stroheim's view of human corruption, societal elegance, and ironic,
comic details in such films as *Foolish Wives* (1922) and *The Merry
Widow* (1925) looks forward to Renoir's *Rules of the Game*.
Renoir admits to being heavily influenced by von Stroheim's work.
And one recalls that von Stroheim plays a leading role in *Grand
Illusion,* made shortly before *The Rules of the Game*.

The success of *The Rules of the Game* at being both sad and
silly at the same time is at least partly responsible for the controversy
about the film and the incomplete interpretations of it that abound.
The satirical sting—the devastating reduction of human beings to
silly clowns—is striking and obvious, and undoubtedly provoked the
hostility of French film audiences when the film premiered. 1939
was a poor year for reducing human effort to nonsense. But the
tendency to see the film as a purely satirical indictment of a corrupt

social system dominates the reviews written since the reconstructed print of the film appeared in 1959.

Eugene Archer of the *New York Times* (January 19, 1961) saw André Jurieu as the film's innocent hero who "broke the rules of a society founded upon superficial manners by revealing the sincerity of his emotions." P.V.B. in the *New York Herald-Tribune* (January 19, 1961) called the film a "satire on French society" and a "sharp criticism of social pretenses." Archer Winsten of the *New York Post* (January 23, 1961) saw it "showing the corruption of French society from top to bottom."

The more intellectual critics have responded similarly. According to Penelope Gilliatt (*The New Yorker,* September 20, 1969), "Society is satirized in it with Mozart's own mixture of biting good sense and blithe, transforming acceptance." But what happens to satire and its bite when accompanied by "acceptance?" She realizes that the film is "delicately good to every character in it, even the most spoiled or stilted," but she does not develop the tension between this "delicate goodness" and satire's moral condemnation. John Simon (*Private Screenings,* pp. 22–24) pins a "moral" on the film: "When a society is shot through with infidelities and jealousies, the relatively noble are apt to pay the price for the ignoble." But what society is not? Is the film only about French society? Simon later suspects that the film is "an attack, perhaps, on the excesses of private property," a generalization that seems irrelevant to the chases of love and death.

For Andrew Sarris (*The American Cinema,* p. 74), the film is "an elaboration of the class structure as seen from the multiple viewpoint." For Pauline Kael (*Kiss Kiss Bang Bang,* p. 430), "The mores are just convenient manners. . . . Charm is more important than feeling." And I fear that I have also done violence to the film (in *A Short History of the Movies,* p. 260) in the interest of baring its soul with brevity: "Both masters and servants value good form over sincerity and the open expression of human emotion. The inevitable result is death." All of these interpretations beg the question because the key descriptive terms—sincerity, social form, emotions, superficial manners, infidelities, convenient—contain their own moral assumptions that are not necessarily warranted by the film.

Although most critics feel confident about Renoir's social statement, they have been much more confused about the film's tone.
Pauline Kael (in *I Lost It at the Movies,* p. 174) correctly calls the
film "a great satirical comedy, a dance of death" in the same sen-
tence, without examining the ironic and complex consequences of
such a mixture. John Simon claims, "What begins and develops as
high comedy ends tragically." He notes that the film disproves the
maxim, "Thou shalt not change tone at the end of the film." Yet
the film does not change tone at the end. The grimness that surfaces
in the final section has accompanied and muted the comic action
from the film's beginning. The "high comedy" in the film is not
very high and not very comic; there are no whoops of laughter in
an audience at even the film's most frantic moments. And there is
no deep tragedy at its climax either; the cold, distant irony mutes
the sorrow at the end, just as it muted the gaiety of the early sections. The film's tone is consistent throughout. It both begins and
ends with a public ceremony outdoors at night.

The difficulties of the film's meaning and tone are inseparable
and identical, which leads to the difficulty of answering two important critical questions about Renoir's artistic intentions slighted
by reviewers. First, what is Renoir really saying about people,
society, the rules and the game? The film's tone makes it impossible
to identify or empathize with any character (and, hence, with any
character's values or choices) to the exclusion of another. All of
them seem to have their touching moments as well as their moments
of buffoonery. Second, what then does the film affirm about human
experience? Many critics prefer *Grand Illusion* to *Rules of the
Game,* probably because the earlier film's characters are more
committed and less foolish; eventually two of them succeed at
accomplishing something. The positive human values in *Grand
Illusion* are much clearer and more sharply defined (the German
farm where Maréchal and Rosenthal find refuge).

What is clear about *The Rules of the Game* is that Renoir takes
special care to make nothing seem clear. That the film's structure
is as complex and careful as a watch is obvious. Nothing in the film
is accidental; everything counts; every event and character parallels
or contrasts with some other event and character. The film is a
completely controlled and totally integrated artistic universe. But

within that universe Renoir handles his parallels and contrasts very complexly. It is not simply that Schumacher parallels Robert as a husband, André parallels Marceau as a "poacher," and Lisette parallels Christine as a siren. At other points in the film, André parallels Robert as jealous "husband," Geneviève parallels André as "poacher," Schumacher parallels Marceau as man of the outdoors, Octave parallels Lisette as "servant," Octave parallels Marceau as "poacher," and so on and on and on. No single definition or term applies to any figure, because the characters shift their behavior according to the circumstances. Two characters who seemed most opposed at one moment of the film seem very alike at another, and two who seemed very alike at one moment seem totally different at another. That kind of complexity of structure and character produces a very rich and complicated work of art but does not lead very easily to constructing a paradigm of the film's moral values.

Who is morally superior to whom in the film? What actions are morally superior to others? The answers to such questions would reveal not only what Renoir is saying in the film but what he affirms as well. Those questions can be rephrased into a simpler and more specific one. Who is responsible for the death of André Jurieu? His death is clearly the film's tragic deed. How could it have been avoided?

One obvious answer is that the rules of the game are themselves responsible, that to reduce spontaneous human emotions to a pre-scribed series of social amenities is deadly; it converts the quick into the dead both metaphorically and literally. There is ample evidence in the film for such an interpretation. Robert's society functions by its formal rules and etiquette, primarily the golden rule that nothing should be said aloud in public about what is taking place in private, that personal emotions should never interfere with the order and unity of the society as a whole. The deadliness of such a rule is evident in Robert's mechanical birds, dolls, and music boxes which have substituted order and regularity for vitality and spontaneity. It is evident in the murderous hunt during which the hunters, using the etiquette, order, and precision of their society's assumptions, turn living rabbits and pheasants into corpses. When the romantic André decides to play by the rules of Robert's order instead of fleeing immediately with Christine, he signs his own death warrant. Octave also contributes his signature when, upon his return to the chateau from the greenhouse, he heeds its rules and assumptions. To a certain extent, the death of André is merely an extension of the death of the rabbits—murdered by a social system they can neither comprehend nor observe.

Although these implications certainly exist in the film, Renoir also qualifies them. If one can say that the rules of the game cause André's death, one can also say that violating the rules causes that death. It is equally possible to interpret the film not as an attack on society but on the chaotic human passions that threaten society. Although the rabbits are spontaneous and alive, they damage the works of men. Although Robert's birds are not alive, they do not harm anyone. Every time a character acts from passion, he destroys one of the necessities of civilization—André's opening confession on the radio threatens Robert's relationship with Christine; Robert's brawl with André threatens both their friendship and the emotional loyalties of everyone in that house; Schumacher's brawl with Marceau threatens the lives of Robert's guests. André dies not because someone observes the rules of the game but because someone does not. Schumacher turns his internal, private passion into an overt public act (just as André did in the film's first sequence). The force that murders André is precisely the force that makes him different from all those who play the game by the rules.

A third complicating influence on an interpretation of the film's values is the presence of time. The catastrophe of *The Rules of the Game* occurs at a precise moment in history, a moment when the traditional order of the past is distintegrating and only chaos seems to be taking its place. The film purposely poses a contrast between the order of the eighteenth century—the chateau, the mechanical music boxes, Mozart—and the chaos of the twentieth—Germany, anti-Semitism, the automobile, radio, telephone, and airplane. To prefer the stability of the old order to the terrifying instability of the new disorder is both human and understandable. It is also, unfortunately, an anachronism, and, therefore, a human impossibility. Robert and his society are merely sticking a finger in a leaky dam, holding a flood that cannot possibly be restrained and will certainly engulf them. But what else can Robert and Christine do? *"Après moi, le déluge."* The sentiment may not be admirable but it makes a great deal of human and psychological sense. And this implied sentiment in the film unmistakably links the work with both Beaumarchais and Mozart, who were contemporaries of the king who originally uttered the famous line.

There is simply no way to reconcile the equally valid and completely contradictory facts of the film itself. Rather than showing some simple and single cause of the catastrophe, Renoir instead poses the contradiction between the order of society and the chaos of passion, both of which are necessary for human survival, both of which threaten the existence of the other, and neither of which can be excluded from a meaningful life. The human condition for Renoir in this film is a delicate balance between the demands of order and spontaneity. Inevitably, a character drops one necessity to clutch the other exclusively. The result of such a failure is either the destruction of the social whole or the death of the individual spirit. But failure at the balancing act is as inevitable and necessary as the act itself. Man must juggle the two demands and he must also fail to juggle them perfectly for they cannot ever really be juggled perfectly. Robert is the best juggler in the film, revealing both passion and a passion for order. But his final compromise at the end of the film—the acceptance of so many lies for the sake of order —is merely a magnification of the compromises that he inevitably must make throughout the film and his life.

The idea that human beings have been assigned an impossible task at which they are doomed to fail is one of the major components of the film's tone and contributes to the cold, acid current that underlies the farce. Most of Renoir's films confront his characters with the same dilemma, the same conflict between society and nature, the horns of which they manage to avoid in some way or other. In *Boudu sauvé des eaux* Renoir resolves the tension between nature and society by leaving the bourgeois man of society in society and taking the natural man out of it. In *Grand Illusion* the representatives of the polite social order die but the two more natural, spontaneous men escape to a new ilfe and a new, more hopeful social order. In *The Golden Coach* and *French Cancan* the world of art synthesizes and replaces the demands of nature and society. But in *The Rules of the Game* Renoir impales his characters squarely on the horns of the dilemma, and the result is both deceit and death.

Nor do the characters fail with particular nobility or courage. They fail stupidly and clownishly. Unlike the classical tragedy which depicts the inevitability of human failure without stripping the human effort to avoid failure of its dignity, Renoir's tragic farce laughs not only at the results but at the effort itself. The characters are ridiculously out of touch with their own actions; they are hardly conscious of the lies they tell and the suffering they cause. Robert does not truly become conscious of the contradiction between sincerity and society even at the end of the film; throughout the film he unconsciously embodies that very contradiction by applying one set of values to his wife's interest in André and another to his own affair with Geneviève. Octave is most conscious of his own failure as a sincere and committed human being; he knows he has become a mere pawn in the social game and that he is dependent on it for survival. But his consciousness of his own failure does not prevent him from failing as badly (or worse) than anybody else. Despite his self-awareness Octave is still a clown—oafish, cowardly, sluggish, a lumbering bear.

Renoir takes care to make comic buffoons of almost all his characters at some point. Robert drops his dignity for a petulant brawl with André; there is also his childishly comic love for his mechanical pets. Geneviève has her screaming fits and Jackie her fainting spells. Even the icily dignified Schumacher becomes one of the prime participants in the comic chase. To reduce these passionate humans to buffoons (the typical device of comedy) is also to reduce their passionate activity to nonsense, even if the nonsense is really related to the most serious questions of life and death, manners and morality, love and friendship. Renoir's comedy seems so black and his revelry so grim precisely because he has not only depicted human failure to be inevitable, but he has not even allowed his characters a Pyrrhic victory in their manner of failing.

Viewed in such a way, it is difficult to see *The Rules of the Game* as affirming anything about human conduct or the human condition. Except perhaps that the humans—some of them anyway —try not to fail, even if they don't try very well. Perhaps something affirmative about the film emerges by comparing it with the works of another filmmaker who works with a similar theme and is even less sympathetic toward human effort. Stanley Kubrick also posits a contradiction between civilized, social behavior and natural, spontaneous passions. But Kubrick always equates those passions with animal behavior. His characters do not love; at the most they lust. And they usually do not lust after other human beings but for power over them.

In *Doctor Strangelove* man's societies and governments are mere camouflage for murderous instincts; they really want to drop that atomic bomb. The bomb (and warfare, and the airplane) are merely sexual surrogates—as the constant sexual imagery of that film makes quite clear. In *2001* Kubrick's essential image of men, despite their sophisticated machines, is of the first apeman who converts a tool into an instrument of warfare. And in *A Clockwork Orange* society is so sterile that it forces the natural animal in man to acts of vicious and sadistic brutality. Compared to such maniacs as Dr. Strangelove, Alex, and even Hal, Robert de la Chesnaye's blundering efforts at social order and personal happiness are admirable indeed.

Unlike Kubrick, Renoir shows that men are not animals. The very desire for order is what separates Robert from the rabbits on his grounds. Renoir's characters are capable—or think they are capable—of love. If there is one possible affirmation in *The Rules of the Game* it is the power of love. But once again the film is ambiguous in its treatment of love. Love may be simply one more illusion that Renoir farcically deflates. And this possibility returns us once again to the character of Christine, the film's goddess of love, and the performance of Nora Grégor.

Unlike the other characters in the film, Christine never loses her dignity. But there is also something inhuman and dead about her distant, cold hauteur. Though she tells two characters that she loves them, and she acts as if she feels something for two others, she does not give the impression that she feels anything at all. Is her perfectly dignified coldness intentional or merely the result of the director's inability to elicit any warm responses from his actress?

In Renoir's defense, it must be said that whatever problems the actress may have caused him, her performance in the film never seems bad or inadequate. It merely seems strange and disturbing. Why do all those men care about her? To some extent, the answer seems to be that they do because they do. Like Marceau's immediate attraction to Lisette, the men seem attracted to Christine because of something within themselves not because of something about her. Perhaps the stone statue of the goddess of love in François Truffaut's *Jules and Jim* is a revealing parallel. The men in *The Rules of the Game* seem to project their own fancies and desires onto a woman of stone. That the woman does not seem worthy or capable of inspiring desire is irrelevant to her suitors.

It is relevant, however, to an interpretation of the film's ultimate statement and intentions, for if love is the force that produces the chaotic catastrophe, and if love seems as ambiguous and as foolish as so many of the other actions and events in the film, then how affirmative is Renoir's treatment of human love? In the film that finally resulted from this structure and with this actress (and the film is the only basis for judging Renoir's intentions), love seems no more (nor less) meaningful a human pursuit than mechanical dolls, the slaughter of rabbits, or even the death of a hero.

The Rules of the Game depicts the failure of love, the failure of society, and the failure of men to rise above the ridiculous. Their only success is that they try and they care. If such a gloomy premise can serve as the basis for a masterpiece of film art, it is perhaps because the film (like the greatest classical tragedies) makes us aware of the painful consequences of our own mortality and does so with masterful artistic control: of a complex multilevel structure, a visual style that mirrors the action and ideas by working with contrasts of light and dark, a unique tone that plays comedy and despair against one another, and a perception of human psychology that never allows human aspirations to fall into easy and schematic categories and clichés.

a Renoir filmography
bibliography
rental source

a Renoir filmography

1924   *La Fille de L'eau*
1926   *Nana*
1927   *Sur un air de Charleston*
       Marquita
1928   *La Petite marchande d'allumettes* (*The Little Match Girl*)
       Tire-au-flanc
1929   *Le Tournoi dans la cité*
       Le Bled
       Le Petit Chaperon Rouge (co-directed with Alberto Cavalcanti)
1931   *On Purge bébé*
       La Chienne
1932   *La Nuit du carrefour*
       Boudu sauvé des eaux (*Boudu Saved from Drowning*)
1933   *Chotard et compagnie*
1934   *Madame Bovary*
1935   *Toni*
1936   *The Crime of Monsieur Lange*
       La Vie est à nous
       Une partie de campagne (*A Day in the Country*)
       Les Bas-fonds (*The Lower Depths*)
1937   *Grand Illusion*
1938   *La Marseillaise*
       La Bête humaine
1939   *La Règle du jeu* (*The Rules of the Game*)
1941   *Swamp Water*
1943   *This Land is Mine*
1944   *Salute to France* (co-directed with Garson Kanin)
1945   *The Southerner*
1946   *The Diary of a Chambermaid*
1947   *The Woman on the Beach*
1951   *The River*
1953   *Le Carosse d'or* (*The Golden Coach*)
1955   *French Cancan*
1956   *Elena et les hommes*
1959   *Le Déjeuner sur l'herbe* (*Picnic on the Grass*)

1961   *The Testament of Dr. Cordelier*
1962   *Le Caporal Épinglé (The Elusive Corporal)*
1970   *Le Petit Théâtre de Jean Renoir*

bibliography

I. BOOKS ON JEAN RENOIR

Bazin, André. *Jean Renoir* (Paris: Éditions Champs Libre, 1971), ed. François Truffaut.
> A collection of Bazin essays on Renoir and notes for an unpublished book.
Braudy, Leo. *Jean Renoir: The World of His Films* (Garden City, N.Y.: Doubleday, 1972).
> A thematic study of Renoir's work.
Cauliez, Armand-Jean. *Jean Renoir* (Paris: Éditions Universitaires, 1962).
> A collection of critical statements, interviews, biographical studies, organized chronologically.
Chardère, Bernard. *Jean Renoir* (Lyon: Premier Plan, 1962).
> A collection of interviews, details of production, anecdotal recollections, organized by film.
Leprohon, Pierre. *Jean Renoir* (New York: Crown, 1971).
> A collection of critical views, screenplay excerpts, and personal recollections, translated from the French.

II. RENOIR'S OWN STATEMENTS—INTERVIEWS AND WRITINGS

Cahiers du Cinéma, 8 (January 1952).
> Issue devoted to interviews with and statements by Renoir.
Cahiers du Cinéma, 78 (Christmas 1957).
> Issue devoted to interviews with and articles on Renoir.
Interviews with Film Directors, ed. Andrew Sarris. (New York: Bobbs-Merrill, 1967). "Interview with Louis Marcorelles." Originally published in *Sight and Sound.*

Renoir, Jean. "The Filmmaker and the Audience." In *Film: Book 1*, ed. Robert Hughes (New York: Grove Press, 1959). Renoir examines replies to a questionnaire.

Renoir, Jean. *Renoir, My Father* (Boston: Little, Brown, 1962). Famous son examines once more-famous father.

Renoir, Jean. *The Rules of the Game* (New York: Simon and Schuster, 1969). The screenplay also includes interviews with the director and a critical article on the film.

Rivette, Jacques. "Entretien avec Jean Renoir," *Cahiers du Cinéma,* 34 (April 1954), 3–22; continued in 35 (May 1954), 14–30.

III. ARTICLES ON AND REVIEWS OF THE RULES OF THE GAME

A. Reviews (selected)

Financial Times (London), September 29, 1961.

New York Herald-Tribune, January 19, 1961.

New York Post, January 23, 1961.

New York Times, January 19, 1961.

Variety, August 30, 1939.

B. Articles and pieces

Cowie, Peter. *Seventy Years of Cinema* (New York: Barnes, 1969), 129.

Gilliatt, Penelope. "Game Without Umpire," *The New Yorker,* Sept. 20, 1969, 150ff.

Joly, J. "Between Theatre and Life: Jean Renoir and *The Rules of the Game,*" *Film Quarterly,* 21: 2 (Winter 1967–68), 2–9.

Kael, Pauline. *Kiss Kiss Bang Bang* (Boston: Little, Brown, 1965), 341–43.

Simon, John. *Private Screenings* (New York: Macmillan, 1967), 22–24.

Tyler, Parker. *Classics of the Foreign Film: A Pictorial Treasury* (New York: Citadel Press, 1962), 130–35.

IV. ARTICLES AND DISCUSSIONS OF RENOIR'S CAREER IN GENERAL

Armes, Roy. *French Cinema Since 1946. 1.* (New York: Barnes, 1966), 35–44. Renoir's post-war films as continuing the pre-war tradition.

Bazin, André. "En abordant le théâtre à soixante ans Jean Renoir a voulu recommencer à zéro," *Arts,* 508 (March 1955), 23–29.

Renoir's experience with his play, *Orvet.*

Beranger, Jean. "Portrait de Jean Renoir," *Cahiers de l'écran,* 1, 1947, 5–16.

Beranger, Jean. "The Illustrious Career of Jean Renoir," *Yale French Studies,* 17 (Summer 1956), 27–37.

Cahiers de l'écran. "Table chronologique du films principals," 1, 1947, 3.

Callenbach, Ernest and Schuldenfrei, Roberta, "The Presence of Jean Renoir," *Film Quarterly,* 14:2 (Winter 1960), 8–10.

Carey, Gary. "The Renoir Experience," *Seventh Art,* 1:3, 16–17, 27–28.

Ciné-Club. "L'oeuvre de Jean Renoir," 6 (April 1948), 6–7.

Dyer, Peter John, "Renoir and Realism," *Sight and Sound,* 29:3 (Summer 1960), 130–135.

Écran Français. "Jean Renoir," 159 (July 13, 1948), 2.

Gilliatt, Penelope. "Le Meneur de Jeu," *The New Yorker,* August 23, 1969, 34–61.

On the Renoir retrospective at the New York Film Festival.

Houston, Penelope. *The Contemporary Cinema* (London & Baltimore: Penguin, 1963), 84–86.

Brief summary of Renoir's career and importance to the French tradition.

Institut des hautes études cinématographiques. *Fiche filmographique # 30* (Paris, 1948).

Booklet of films, selected reviews, interviews, and notes.

Mast, Gerald. *The Comic Mind: A View of Comedy and the Movies* (New York: Bobbs-Merrill, 1973).

A chapter on Renoir's comic films and comic style.

Miller, Daniel, "The Autumn of Jean Renoir," *Sight and Sound,* 37:3 (Summer 1968), 136–41, 161.

On the late Renoir films.

Ray, Satyajit, "Renoir in Calcutta," *Sequence,* 10 (New Year 1950), 146–50.

On the filming of *The River.*

Rivette, Jacques, "Renoir in America," *Sight and Sound,* 24:1 (July–September 1954), 12–17.

   On Renoir's American period.

Rohmer, Eric, "Jeunesse de Jean Renoir," *Cahiers du Cinéma,* 102 (December 1959), 1–7.

Sarris, Andrew. *The American Cinema* (New York: Dutton, 1968), 73–74.

   Renoir in the Pantheon of *auteurs.*

rental source

The film is available for rental from Janus Films, 745 Fifth Avenue, New York City, N.Y. 10022, telephone 212 753–7100.